W9-CTL-185

FEMINIST THEOLOGY

GUIDES TO THEOLOGY

Sponsored by the Christian Theological Research Fellowship

EDITORS

Sally Bruyneel • *University of Durham*

Alan G. Padgett • *Luther Seminary*

David A. S. Fergusson • *University of Edinburgh*

Iain R. Torrance • *University of Aberdeen*

Systematic theology is undergoing a renaissance. Conferences, journal articles, and books give witness to the growing vitality of the discipline. The Christian Theological Research Fellowship is one sign of this development. To stimulate further study and inquiry into Christian doctrine, we are sponsoring, with the William B. Eerdmans Publishing Company, a series of readable and brief introductions to theology.

This series of Guides to Theology is written primarily with students in mind. We also hope that pastors, church leaders, and theologians will find them to be useful introductions to the field. Our aim is to provide a brief introduction to the chosen field, followed by an annotated bibliography of important works, which should serve as an entrée to the topic. The books in this series will be of two kinds. Some volumes, like *The Trinity*, will cover standard theological *loci*. Other volumes will be devoted to various modern approaches to Christian theology as a whole, such as feminist theology or liberation theology. The authors and editors alike pray that these works will help further the faithful study of Christian theology in our time.

Visit our Web page at

http://apu.edu/CTRF

FEMINIST THEOLOGY

Natalie K. Watson

WILLIAM B. EERDMANS PUBLISHING COMPANY

GRAND RAPIDS, MICHIGAN / CAMBRIDGE, U.K.

© 2003 Wm. B. Eerdmans Publishing Co.
All rights reserved

Wm. B. Eerdmans Publishing Co.
255 Jefferson Ave. S.E., Grand Rapids, Michigan 49503 /
P.O. Box 163, Cambridge CB3 9PU U.K.

Printed in the United States of America

08 07 06 05 04 03   7 6 5 4 3 2 1

Library of Congress Cataloging-in-Publication Data

ISBN 0-8028-4828-1

www.eerdmans.com

Contents

v

Acknowledgments

At the completion of a book, even a small one like this, there are many people to thank. This list is by no means complete but may the following stand for the many women and men who have accompanied me on my journey of discovery of feminist theology.

Sally Bruyneel and Alan Padgett invited me to contribute to this series when I was still a graduate student.

Ann Loades has been a challenging and creative teacher of feminist theology. Her love for the Christian tradition and for finding new texts in it has been an important challenge without which this book would not have been written.

During the writing of this book, I was reunited with my friend from university days, Christine Meilicke, fellow writer and lover of ideas, through a chance meeting in the Bodleian Library in Oxford. I thank Lena Lybaek for many conversations while we were graduate students. Thanks also to Stephen Barton for inviting me to teach feminist hermeneutics to his students at Durham University. This formed the basis for the sections on scripture in this book.

Yvonne Parrey has often challenged me to be "more feminist." Thanks for friendship and support as this book was written and now as it sees the light of day.

As always, I thank my parents for their encouragement and support. This book is dedicated to them with gratitude.

Introduction

As I was marking up the proofs for this book, I was travelling through West Yorkshire on a train. Looking up from my work, my eyes fell on one of the many small village stations. There was a sign pointing to the "General Waiting Room" alongside one inviting visitors into the "Ladies Waiting Room." I was intrigued by this as it seemed so symbolic of how the work of feminist theologians is often perceived. One could speculate about theology being done on this side of the second coming as something like a waiting room, a space where we sit, talk, and wait for the train to arrive, for the last things to begin. Yet, why is there a general one and one for ladies? Are women not part of the general public?

This book introduces feminist theology. Feminist Theology is not separate "ladies" theology, not an academic luxury while others get on with "the real thing." Feminist theologians seek to make a contribution, to ask critical questions of all endeavours of doing theology. This book is an invitation to take these questions seriously and to see how feminist theology aims to do theology as, for, and with the whole body of Christ.

In doing so, Scripture and Tradition have been dialogue partners which are too vital to ignore. Feminist Theology looks at a wide range of themes in Christian theology and the language used to discuss them. It invites its readers to rejoice in the diversity of voices in today's theological landscape and shows how theology done by the whole body of Christ cannot ignore the human bodies of women and men if it wants to be true to Christ incarnate. There are many feminist theologies, a diversity of bodies and voices, waiting to be heard, listening to each other and engaging critically with the Christian tradition.

The first part of the book outlines and discusses some of the ideas of feminist theologians in their creative, critical, and constructive dialogues with Scripture and the Christian Tradition. The second part invites the reader to look at the work of some feminist theologians in more detail through an annotated bibliography. The list of books in the annotated bibliography and the topics discussed in the first two chapters are by no means exhaustive. They indicate a place to begin, to start a journey of discovery. As it sometimes happens on journeys, the waiting room may become a place of unexpected, challenging encounters. . . .

1. Scripture and Tradition

In the course of its development, Christian theology has undergone a number of shifts in perspective with regard to what theology is and what theologians talk about. The Enlightenment at the end of the seventeenth century put *human beings* and their experience on the intellectual agenda. With this, theology could no longer be understood as an abstract and "objective science," but had to take adequate account of its "subjective" dimension. One aspect of this can be seen in the emphasis that contemporary theology has placed upon context and the role of communal experience in theological reflection. For example, in the 1970s and 80s, the work of Black American and Latin American theologians made clear that there were indeed many different "worlds" within the one world. The realization that no single community could definitively address the theological task challenged the way theology had been done so far: doing theology had to take place where people lived, and advocate the issues that arose from their particular lives.

The challenge of liberation theology was not only to take into account the perspectives of those doing theology, but also to look more closely at the life and experience of marginalized and oppressed people. The change in perspective advocated by liberation theologians required us to ask how justice can be done through theology and through the life of the church. It was about this time that feminist theologians began to make themselves heard. They argued that something else was missing from the agenda of theology: theology had overlooked the existence and the lives of *women*. In addition, they made clear many of the ways that this sacred discipline had

1

been used as an instrument to silence and oppress women. Not only was women's experience denigrated or excluded as a source of theological reflection, but women were forced to assume a "male" perspective if they wanted to be involved in the task of doing theology.

Introduction: What Is Feminist Theology?

So what *is* feminist theology? There are two dimensions to doing feminist theology: critical *analysis* and constructive *re-reading and re-writing* that involves a commitment to transformation. In this respect we say that feminist theology is

> critical,
> contextual,
> constructive,
> creative.

Feminist theologians analyze the situation of women in church and society, past and present. This critical analysis is not restricted to those theological texts that deal explicitly with women or are written by women, but it is concerned with *all* texts, and in fact all aspects of life, as they create and shape the situation of women. This may be done either by speaking explicitly about women, or by denying the existence of women and the relevance of women's lives for doing theology.

As a second step, feminist theologians develop new ways of reading the history of the church and all theological texts from the perspective of women. In feminist theology, women assume their place as both readers and authors of theology. In so doing, feminist theologians re-frame the theological debate by expanding the range of areas that theologians study. Appropriate reflection should not be limited to academic texts, but should also take account of women's lives and experiences, as well as different types of women's spiritualities, both traditional and new. As we explore what this means, I propose the following working definition of feminist theology:

> Feminist theology is the critical, contextual, constructive, and creative re-reading and re-writing of Christian theology. It regards women — and their bodies, perspectives, and experiences — as rel-

evant to the agenda of Christian theologians and advocates them as subjects of theological discourses and as full citizens of the church.

It is important to realize from the outset that the goal of feminist theology is not merely the inclusion of some feminist ideas into otherwise unchanged structures, or the admission of women theologians to the arenas in which theology is done. Feminist theology does not seek to be one more voice represented at the table of patriarchy. Neither does it advocate the complete separation of women from men. Feminist theologians aim instead at the transformation of theological concepts, methods, language, and imagery into a more holistic theology as a means and an expression of the struggle for liberation. This involves an awareness of the ambivalence that many of the symbols and texts within the Christian tradition create for women. It implies the ability to respond to this ambivalence, not by discarding the key symbols of Christianity altogether, but by identifying *dis*-empowering readings of them and constructing and proposing new readings that advocate the full humanity of women.

Feminist theologians are in constant dialogue with the Christian tradition. This dialogue can take a variety of different forms. Some feminist theologians try to reconcile Christianity and feminism by arguing that Christianity, read in the right way, advocates equality and justice in the same way that feminism does. The American theologian Leonard Swidler, for example, argues that "Jesus was a feminist." Representatives of this particular form of Christian feminism may be found in the work of Denise Lardner Carmody, and in some of the early writings of Virginia Ramey Mollenkott. The Christian tradition becomes a resource for feminists who find the values they advocate — the full humanity of women and their equality with men — inherent within the Christian tradition, but also distorted through patriarchal thinking. Feminist theology and the Christian tradition are therefore means of a mutual critique, enabling a more holistic form of doing theology for both women and men.

Other feminist theologians advocate a radically new reading of Christian theology. This new reading understands women's experiences and the full humanity of women as the criterion by which all theology has to be judged. Some texts within the Christian tradition are regarded as usable, while others are not. Therefore the search for such "usable texts" has to be extended beyond the boundaries of Christianity itself. The most prominent writers of this second group are Rosemary Radford Ruether and Elis-

3

abeth Schüssler Fiorenza. Fiorenza, for example, argues that the Bible can no longer be understood as the authoritative source for women, as an archetype of Christian belief, but must rather be seen as a resource for women's struggle for liberation. In other words, as a text the Bible portrays a movement of equality, justice, and liberation that can be seen as a prototype and inspiration for women today.

Rosemary Radford Ruether identifies five areas of such "usable traditions." These are: Scripture, marginalized or "heretical" traditions within Christianity, the primary theological themes within the mainstream of Christian theology, non-Christian Near-Eastern and Greco-Roman religion and philosophy, and critical post-Christian worldviews such as liberalism, romanticism, or Marxism. The ultimate criterion by which any tradition or text is to be judged is whether or not it manages to promote the full humanity of women and thereby advocates women's struggle for liberation from male oppression. We can here distinguish between feminist theologies that advocate equality between women and men, and feminist theologies that focus specifically on women. Representatives of the latter group ask: Who are the women about whom feminist theology speaks?

It is important to remember that feminist theologians do not necessarily have to be women. In fact, there are a number of male theologians who have taken on board feminist concerns, for example, the British hymn writer and theologian Brian Wren and the German theologian Jürgen Moltmann. Moreover, not all female theologians are feminist theologians; some of them use methods of patriarchal scholarship uncritically. As the black feminist Audre Lorde has argued, "the master's tools will not dismantle the master's house." Put another way, uncritical participation in oppressive structures leads to a perpetuation of those structures. In keeping with this perspective, some feminist theologians have given up fighting for the ordination of women. They view women being ordained to the priesthood in a patriarchal church as driving a division among women by sustaining the existing patriarchal structures rather than transforming the church into a liberated cohumanity.

Feminist Ways of Reading Scripture

Feminist theologians engage with the key sources of Christian theology such as Scripture, the history of Christian thought, and traditional approaches to doing theology. In this section we will consider feminist approaches to the most important text of Christianity, the Bible. The Bible is the key text for Christians, and one of our primary ways of knowing about God. However, over the centuries the Bible has been a source of ambivalent messages for women: some texts within the Hebrew Bible and the Christian Testament have been sources of hope and empowerment, while others, such as St. Paul's command for women to be silent in the church, have been used to exclude women from the main aspects of the church and to deny them their full citizenship in the life of the church. While some feminists have chosen to reject the Bible on the grounds of its history and potential for abuse, for most feminist theologians, the Bible remains a force to be reckoned with.

Feminist theology is concerned with reading and interpreting Scripture and the Christian tradition in the light of women's experiences. The aim of such a re-reading is to un-cover women's absences as well as to discover women's presences throughout the history of the Christian church and in those texts the Christian church considers relevant and normative. In this context, feminist biblical hermeneutics is the process of developing a critical and constructive reading of Scripture that advocates women as full members of the Christian church. However, the feminist theologians of the twentieth century were not the first women to read the scriptures of the Hebrew and the Christian Testaments in order to make sense of them for their own situations. A number of women could be mentioned, including St. Paula and St. Eustochium, who worked with St. Jerome on the translation of the scriptures into Latin. Medieval nuns were often literate and were both readers and interpreters of Scripture.

The Reformation in the sixteenth and seventeenth century saw the "rediscovery of Scripture" as it proclaimed its *sola scriptura* (through Scripture alone) and advocated not only the distinction between Scripture and tradition, but also the reading of Scripture by lay people. Luther and his fellow Reformers advocated the importance of literacy and education, which for Luther also included the education of women. One of them was Argula von Grumbach, born in 1492 in Bavaria. From an early age, her family encouraged her, despite the warnings of some of their spiritual advisers, to read and study the Bible. A number of her male relatives, who looked after her when her parents died of the plague while Argula was still in her teens, were involved in the Reformation. She herself spent some time as a lady in waiting at the court in Munich. In 1516 or 1517, the year in

5

which Luther hammered his ninety-five theses on the door of the Schlosskirche in Wittenberg, Argula married Friedrich von Grumbach with whom she had four children before he died in 1530. In Ingolstadt in southwest Germany, Argula von Grumbach first came in contact with some of the theological ideas of the Wittenberg Reformers.

Argula von Grumbach later corresponded with Luther and also encouraged the nobility of her native Bavaria to take on the ideas of the Reformers. Both Argula and her husband came under suspicion, and it was suggested that she should have two fingers amputated to stop her from writing. Von Grumbach tried to promote the cause of the Reformation both through the writing of pamphlets and through her extensive travels around southwest Germany. In doing that, Argula broke a number of taboos. She assumed a public role, which was unheard of for a woman of her time. It was more than a public role, it was that of a theological writer and exegete of Scripture. Von Grumbach read Scripture both as a "coherent, unitary and certain revelation of God's prevenient grace in Christ" and as a book of ordinances for all aspects of both ecclesial and social life.

The combination of the two suggests an original approach, which uses some of the ideas of the Reformers, yet takes them in a different direction. She argued strongly for the independence of the church from secular authority when it came to spiritual matters such as the understanding of the Eucharist. Scripture for Argula von Grumbach was furthermore a challenge to confession. It is God's living word that generates life out of chaos. The latter is linked with a strong apocalyptic dimension in von Grumbach's theology. Von Grumbach understood herself as called and led by the Spirit of God to read and understand the scriptures. Aware of the apostle Paul's advice for women not to speak or teach in public, von Grumbach understood herself as a prophetess. After the early death of her husband, who had not been entirely supportive, Argula remarried, but her second husband as well as three of her four children died relatively early. Only one of her sons would outlive her death in 1554.

A more recent key figure in the development of "feminist hermeneutics" was the Quaker Elizabeth Cady Stanton, the compiler of *The Woman's Bible*. Stanton's project comprised a proposed revision of those texts in the Bible that referred directly to women and their immediate concerns. Her collection of short commentaries was conceived as a means in the struggle for women's equality. Stanton and her cowriters saw the roots of women's inequality (as it was expressed, for example, in the denial of the vote to women and the fact that married women had no individual right to own property), as deeply rooted in a Western civilization that in turn was based on the Judeo-Christian tradition proposed in the Hebrew and Christian scriptures. Institutional Christianity, she argued, had created and supported the supposed inferiority of women, which was not in line with Jesus' message of equality. Elizabeth Cady Stanton had been very involved in the movements for women's equality and liberation in the second half of the nineteenth century. Together with Lucretia Mott, a Quaker feminist, she was involved in the first convention for women's rights at Seneca Falls in 1848. Stanton saw women's suffrage as an important goal for the women's rights movement, yet she argued that it was but a step forward towards the full emancipation of women.

Although Elizabeth Cady Stanton and her contemporaries have been criticized by later feminist readers for their identification of feminism with the concerns of white propertied women, Stanton did envisage the women's movement as including women from a variety of different backgrounds. It was to be a platform for dialogue between women of different religious and political persuasions. In her theological and exegetical work, Stanton argued that any interpretation of Scripture by male theologians and clerics was essentially flawed as it was based on the false premise of female inferiority and male domination. She further distinguished between religion and theology. While the latter was an institutionalized activity on which men had for centuries claimed to hold the monopoly, religion was a reasonable activity that meant accepting the divine order, which was indeed just and reasonable.

Theology was a tainted enterprise, while religion was from God. Stanton wrote:

> The canon law, the Scriptures, the creeds and codes and church discipline of the leading religions bear the impress of fallible man, and not of our ideal great first cause, "the Spirit of all Good," that set the universe of matter and mind in motion, and by immutable law holds the land, the sea, the planets, revolving round the great centre of light and heat, each in its own elliptic, with millions of stars in harmony all singing together, the glory of creation forever and ever.[1]

1. Elizabeth Cady Stanton, *The Women's Bible* (Edinburgh: Polygon Books, 1985), p. 13.

Unlike Argula von Grumbach, who saw her interpretation of Scripture very much as her own vocation, Elizabeth Cady Stanton believed that it was time for women to take up their own right to read and interpret Scripture. To exercise this right would in fact mean an important step towards women's equality in both church and society. Not surprisingly perhaps, Stanton's critical approach to Scripture encountered a great deal of opposition from male church leaders. She was likewise opposed by other women, who saw a critical approach to the Bible as ultimately detrimental to the cause of women's independence and liberation. Women like Argula von Grumbach and Elisabeth Cady Stanton are important landmarks in the history of women's reading of Scripture as women. They were, however, not feminist theologians or engaged in a feminist reading of Scripture as such. Feminist hermeneutics, in the proper sense of the term, did not come into being until the second half of the twentieth century. What, then, is a distinctly feminist reading of Scripture?

In order to understand how feminist theologians understand Scripture, we have to look at three different categories: the reader, the text, and the context. First: Who is *the reader?* For feminist theologians, the reader can no longer be a gender-neutral universal person who reads the biblical text from an "objective" point of view. The answer also cannot simply be: woman (or women). Feminist biblical interpretation is not a reading of the Bible from a woman's perspective, as the category "woman" is itself a highly problematic one. What matters, for the reader, is the significance of being female in a particular situation. What it means to be a woman in a particular situation is always structured by other factors like class, race, or ethnicity. Therefore no reading of sacred texts will ever be solely from a woman's perspective. The reading of sacred texts will, however, be from an *informed* woman's perspective. It will be informed by factors like class, race, or ethnicity. But it is always a reading by someone who has not traditionally been part of the reading community, whose particular voice has not been heard in the process of making sense of the Christian tradition before. Reading from a feminist perspective means reclaiming the authority not only of women, but of all those who are on the "underside," in what feminists call the patriarchal mindset, as readers of Scripture.

It has frequently been pointed out that as courageous and important as it was in her time, Cady Stanton's project was hampered by the fact that her perspective was limited to her white American middle-class mindset. This she claimed to be a "woman's reading" of the Bible. It has been one of the most important movements in the short history of feminist theology that other women have started to reclaim their authority as readers of the Bible as well. A feminist reading of Scripture is therefore a reading that takes account of the particular situation of the reader and the factors that construct it, such as her sex, race, and socio-economic situation. The reading of the text can therefore never be seen in isolation from the situation of the reader. Feminist biblical hermeneutics encourages the reader to make the connection between the biblical text and her own situation, to challenge the text from her own perspective as a woman, and to be challenged by it. Women therefore need to become aware of the extent to which biblical texts have both shaped their lives as women within the Jewish and Christian traditions and how these texts create meaning/make sense for them.

The next central issue is: *the text.* This question divides up into two other questions: Which text? and Why this text? To mark the centenary of the publication of Elizabeth Cady Stanton's *The Woman's Bible,* a two-volume work called *Searching the Scriptures* was published. Even though it marked the centenary of *The Woman's Bible,* it was quite different from it and therefore can serve as an example for the development of feminist hermeneutics. First of all, these two volumes are collections of essays written by a variety of authors rather than one author or a small group of very similar persons. And they are no longer only focused on what we call the canonical scriptures or the Bible. The question to be asked was, What significance does a text that had often been used to justify the subordination of women — not to mention slavery, racism, and war — have for women at the end of the second millennium, struggling for their own liberation and that of society as a whole?

The first step is to acknowledge that the scriptures are a collection of texts chosen by someone else as being relevant for the Christian tradition. This leads to a thorough reconsideration of how the canon of Scripture was compiled in the first place. Who chose which of the many texts written in the first few centuries immediately after the life and death of Jesus were to be regarded as Scripture? What were the criteria according to which these were selected, and who established them? What significance was given to women and their experiences in this process?

The question of the canon — the question of Why this text? as well as Which text? or Whose text is it anyway? — was very important in the early days of feminist biblical interpretation. The Bible, after all, not only contains potentially liberating and empowering texts such as Mary's Song of Praise in Luke 1, but also a variety of texts that condone and encourage a perception of women as men's property and as ready objects of abuse and marginalization. Examples for the latter are the story of Jephthah's sacrifice (Judges 11), or texts from the Levitical law that force the victim of rape to marry the perpetrator.

There are four options. First, we can dispense with the Christian tradition, certainly in its canonical form, altogether. Second, we can "be selective" and cut out those texts that do not promote the full humanity of women as not canonical. Yet, both these options mean surrendering the life-giving tradition of the Christian church to patriarchy and denying the fact that it has given meaning to women throughout its history. Christianity as rooted in the incarnation of Jesus Christ is essentially a historical religion that challenges its participants to a constant and dynamic engagement with all its aspects. It is too vital for women to exclude themselves from it. Third, we also may insist that all texts are to be interpreted in the light of the *whole Bible*. This means reading Scripture as a collection of texts written over a long period of time in a variety of contexts and situations different from our own. There are therefore different layers of meaning and significance within it. Fourth, we can identify the process of canonization as one carried out by a patriarchal church. With that option we can extend the tradition to texts written by women or to parts of the Christian community in which women played a more significant role. Feminist biblical scholars such as Elisabeth Schüssler Fiorenza have largely chosen the last option. It means that a critical reading of Scripture cannot be separated from awareness of its context and of other, extra-canonical texts; the process of canonization is one in which women were, for a variety of reasons, not involved as active participants but as recipients and interpreters, as those who participated in the process of reading and created their own readings which are part of the tradition of the church as a whole.

A further question is that of authority: a feminist hermeneutic has to identify the process of reading as an interactive process between the reader and the text rather than a one-way scientific exploration. Reader and text, both in their particularity, interact as equal partners in a process. This is what takes place in the Bible itself. Feminist theologians identify the Bible as the site of many different voices rather than a source of objective information. The focus in a feminist reading of Scripture is therefore not merely on the content of Scripture as authoritative and normative for the

Christian community; it is focused primarily on the interactive process of reading, a process that creates meaning for those who participate in the Christian community as the people they are.

This also means becoming aware of the fact that large parts of the Bible do *not* mention women, their experiences, or perspectives at all. Carole Fontaine illustrates this with regard to the Psalms, the book of praise for the whole community, used by both Jews and Christians in their worship. She writes:

> I find no psalms that express despair over miscarriage, or seek vindication for the rape or incest survivor. My Psalter contains no thanksgiving psalms specifically aimed at the celebration of the survival of childbirth, no lyric praise for the miracle that takes place with menarche, no attention at all to the various phases of growth and biological change that mark a woman's life. . . .[2]

The question that arises for feminist readers of Scripture is, What authority can biblical texts such as the Psalms, which are the product of a society with patriarchal worldviews, have for women? A feminist interpretation of Scripture assumes that the authority of the biblical text cannot be separated from the authority of women as its critical readers.

Feminist theologians are critical of a positivistic understanding of the canonical text as its starting point. The praxis of the reading community becomes the location in which a critical and constructive reading of Scripture takes place. The critical principle for feminist theologians is not the Bible itself, not the canon, not a "canon within the canon," not even Christ; it lies in the community of women and men who read the Bible and who, through their dialogical imagination, appropriate it for their own liberation.

What then are possible criteria for such a critical feminist reading of Scripture? Elisabeth Schüssler Fiorenza suggests a fourfold approach to reading Scripture:

1. *Suspicion:* texts are not taken at face value; patriarchal interests of authors are analyzed and require a critical response.

---

2. Carole Fontaine, "The Abusive Bible: On the Use of Feminist Method in Pastoral Contexts," in Athalya Brenner and Carole Fontaine, *A Feminist Companion to Reading the Bible: Approaches, Methods and Strategies* (Sheffield: Sheffield Academic Press, 1997), p. 98.

2. *Remembrance,* which moves beyond specific texts on women to reconstruct women's history obscured by male historical consciousness.
3. *Proclamation:* all scriptural texts are assessed and evaluated theologically for their oppressive impact or liberating tendency.
4. *Creative actualization,* which stimulates our creative powers to recall,
   embody, and celebrate the achievements, sufferings, and struggles of
   the biblical women.

Feminist readers are challenged to liberate the biblical text itself from
being a tool that justifies a patriarchal order of church and society and to
transform it into both a locus for the critique of that same order and also a
means of overcoming it. Such a complex hermeneutical strategy shows
that feminist biblical interpretation does not simply ask whether or not a
particular text is acceptable to women or not, but proposes an interactive
and constructive wrestling with the text.

What about historical criticism? There is no unified opinion among
feminist biblical scholars about the use of the historical-critical method.
Feminist scholars argue for understanding historical-critical scholarship
against the cultural and sociopolitical background in which it developed: a
Eurocentric, male mindset, which has no parallel with the experiences of
the different local reading communities of today.

A number of feminist theologians have dispensed with the historical-
critical method altogether. They identify it as too limited and restricting
with respect to the kind of questions that can be asked about a text, and
therefore limiting the multidimensionality of readings advocated by feminist theologians. Others, like Elisabeth Schüssler Fiorenza, have made use
of historical research while at the same time raising suspicion about a too-
positivistic understanding of what historical-critical scholarship claims to
achieve, in other words, the notion of "scientific objectivity." Fiorenza argues that it must be up to women to define what the terms "historical" and
"critical" signify. She engages, rather, in what she calls a process of historical imagination, in order to reconstruct Christian origins. Attention therefore shifts from "what *happened*" to "what is *remembered.*" This means that
the process of reading becomes inseparable from the text. Some feminist
scholars make constructive use of the methods advocated by historical-
critical scholars and use them as safeguards against fundamentalist and
biblicist readings, which disguise rather than enable the possibility of liberation within Christianity. The historical-critical method can therefore

be vital in establishing a critical approach to the text itself, to identify the importance of reading it with awareness of its own context rather than in an absolute and ahistorical way.

Feminist hermeneutics points to the existence of many different reading communities within the one community of the church as the body of Christ. The question arises, however, of how to draw the line between an uncritical deconstructive pluralism and a healthy diversity that can be constructive for the church as a whole. Letty Russell points out that the Christian tradition contains a potentially liberating core that needs to be recovered. Rosemary Radford Ruether calls for the prophetic tradition as a "canon in the canon." Yet the very notion of a fixed canon is as problematic for feminist theologians as the idea of "canonization." Canonization implies a process of restriction and of selection by a dominant group that excludes those who do not belong to it. In other words, the canon of Scripture as a prescribed selection of texts deemed authoritative is seen as the work of a male-dominated patriarchal church from which women were often excluded.

Fiorenza and others have therefore argued for the idea of an "open canon" that includes texts written by women or reflecting women's experiences. In the second volume of *Searching the Scriptures,* Fiorenza has collected a number of short commentaries on texts that were not accepted into the canon of Christian scriptures but reflect the experiences of women in the earliest Christian centuries and were relevant for women's discourses of faith during the formative period of Christianity. A feminist hermeneutic understands itself as creative re-reading. This means that it not only deals with the readings of old texts, of those texts called "tradition," but also with the writing of new texts.

One form that has been used by both Jewish and Christian authors is the *midrash.* The midrash is an imaginative development of a thought or theme suggested by Scripture. For example, a feminist *midrash* might be a re-reading of the story of the sacrifice of Isaac (Genesis 22) from the perspective of his mother Sarah. Sarah's perspective may be that of a woman whose long-awaited only child is supposed to be sacrificed to an angry patriarchal God. The midrash, then, would allow Jewish and Christian women to write themselves into the history and into the texts from which they have so long been excluded.

In our overview of the issues relevant to a feminist reading of Scripture we have yet to consider the third factor in the interactive process of

13

reading: *the context*. There are two contexts to be taken into account: the first is the context of the text itself; the other is the context of the reading and interpreting. Feminist biblical scholars combine the use of historical methods with literary criticism. Historical methods, employed under the auspices of a hermeneutics of suspicion, provide a means to access the immediate context of the text as well as other contexts in which the text has been read and interpreted. Literary critical methods allow the reader to focus on his or her particular reading situation. For example, the reading of an African American woman will significantly differ from that of a white middle-class woman in Western Europe.

In light of the fact that both the Hebrew and Christian scriptures were the product of patriarchal societies and are still being used by groups like the religious right to maintain a patriarchal order that reduces women to their traditionally established roles, the question becomes: Why bother? Marjorie Procter-Smith discusses the issue of "negative texts" such as the rape of Dinah in the Hebrew scriptures or the apostle Paul's order for women to be silent in church. She suggests four ways of reading those more difficult texts:

1. as educational texts, to be explained or interpreted to the congregation;
2. as objects of critique, a form of reading in which the content of the text is not proclaimed but subverted;
3. as subjects of a rite of exorcism;
4. in a rite of lament, "recognizing the power such texts have exerted over women, giving men the opportunity to confess their use of such texts to oppress women and to repent of that use."

What then is the aim of a feminist reading of Scripture? Marjorie Procter-Smith calls for the development of a feminist theology of proclamation for the use of feminist readings of Scripture in a liturgical context. A feminist proclamation takes account of the patriarchal character of the Bible and of the tradition of patriarchal proclamation. At the same time, it is committed to speaking out on behalf of women for their liberation. As Procter-Smith has pointed out, the commitment to women in this case has to take precedence over the commitment to scriptural texts. The concept of feminist biblical hermeneutics is part and parcel of the feminist theological search to find a place for women within the Christian tradition. It is an act of claiming and reclaiming the key text of Christianity, which throughout the history of the church has been both a tool of women's oppression and a means of their empowerment for liberation. Feminist biblical scholars do not claim to resolve this fundamental ambiguity but seek ways of living with it, working creatively and constructively to make sense of Christianity — an essentially open-ended process.

Feminist theology, in the proper sense of the term, has been a relatively recent development. Yet, that does not mean that women have not throughout the history of the Christian church been involved in its life and also, in a variety of senses, in doing "theology." The following historical overview will therefore divide into two sections: before I look at the historical development of feminist theologies in North America and Europe, I will provide a brief overview of some aspects of women's presence and involvement in the history of the Christian church. Such an overview is important as feminist theologians inevitably have to be in critical and creative dialogue with the Christian tradition, and that means engaging with the Christian past and reclaiming women's presence and participation in it.

Women's History and the Development of Feminist Theology

Two preliminary remarks are necessary before such a survey: first, in the space of a short introduction such an overview is inevitably limited. I can only concentrate on a few selected highlights, a limited range of case studies, rather than provide a complete history of women and the church. The other choice I have made is my concentration on the church in the Christian West. Feminism, in the sense in which most feminist theologians understand it, is a discourse that has mainly taken place in the context of the western world of Europe and North America. That does not mean that there are no authors within the Orthodox churches who are interested in and have written about women's concerns. The most prominent of these are Elisabeth Behr-Sigel and Eva Topping. While the work of the former is important for the debate about the ordination of women, the latter has contributed significantly to the study of Orthodox holy women. Yet a feminist dialogue with the wealth of traditions in the Orthodox churches is sadly lacking and remains a task for the future.

The other observation that must be made is a methodological one, and concerns the writing of women's church history. The author of an overview of the presence of women throughout the life of the Christian church is inevitably faced with a tri-lemma. There are at least three different approaches one could take: one could write a history of women's *inclusion* in the life of the church or a history of women's *exclusion* from major aspects of the life of the church. While the latter reduces women to being victims of patriarchal oppression in the church, the former defines women's worth in the church only when it conforms to a particular male agenda. I will therefore propose a third option by providing a selection of case studies of women's involvement in the church that is not limited to those types of presence, spirituality, and activities regarded as worth studying by male-dominated scholarship.

This leads to a further question: What is the Christian tradition with which feminist theologians are in critical, creative, and constructive dialogue? The Christian tradition that feminist theologians study comprises all three aspects, those of inclusion, exclusion, and presence. Feminist theologians investigate the lives of women past and present, but being theologians, they also have to be concerned with the study of texts. They therefore have to develop criteria according to which such texts from the Christian past are critically appraised in a way that women in the church and on its margins may respond to them.

Feminist theologians were not the first women theologians, and deciding what counts as relevant and authoritative tradition and what remains hidden and unmentioned is an important dimension of feminist theology as a critical and creative process. Yet it remains difficult to find out about the history of the church from the perspective of women, as the number of texts actually written by women is limited. On the other hand, most of the women whose lives we encounter in the history of the Christian church would not have understood themselves as feminists; they often lived and worked within a male-dominated world, assumed their role within the expectations the male-dominated world placed on them, and very often had quite a different understanding of the role of women than that expected by feminists at the end of the twentieth century.

Some of the earliest texts of Christian theology by the Fathers of the church frequently contain disparaging comments about women, such as Tertullian's description of women as "the devil's gateway." Feminist theologians such as Elizabeth Schüssler Fiorenza have identified this as a tendency that is contradictory to the equality that women experienced in the teachings of Jesus and his earliest followers. Fiorenza and others, such as the German biblical scholar Luise Schottroff, criticize male-dominated scholarship for advocating ways of reading the Christian scriptures that conceal these tendencies. The first section of this historical overview will therefore feature a number of *prototypes* that are part of the tradition of a church of both men and women in which feminist theologians see themselves.

Texts written by women or advocating women's equality within the church were not taken into account, and those movements in which women played a major role in leadership and development of theology were often marginalized and condemned as heretical. An example is the second-century Montanist movement. Montanists believed in an outpouring of the Spirit that brought about a new form of authoritative prophecy to challenge the church. Two of the main characters around the founder and leader of the movement, Montanus, were the two prophetesses Priscilla and Maximilla. Some scholars have suggested that Priscilla and Maximilla were the true leaders of this movement, and that the mainstream church, even in calling it heretical, had to relate to the name of a male figure. Some understand Montanus as the advocate and facilitator of women's prophetic gifts. What is important, however, is the very fact that women participated equally in the life and ministry of the Montanist movement. This does not make the Montanist movement feminist, but it does say something about what feminist theologians are seeking to recover in their re-reading of the Christian tradition.

A wide variety of studies have shown that women's involvement in the early church was far greater than much traditional scholarship, as well as many of the surviving sources, would have us believe. Women from all layers of society appeared as martyrs for the Christian faith. An example is the slave girl Blandina who plays an important role in the report on the massacre among the Christians in Lyons in 177 CE.

The early church already shows the ambivalent situation in which women were to find themselves throughout the history of the church. Feminist historians have tried to identify an egalitarian tendency in the earliest Christian churches since there is little of this tendency found in the later stages of church history. This is due to the formation of firmer church-leadership structures in the later development of the church. The institutionalization of the church lowered the role of women's participation in two key ways. First was in the development of a theology of Christian ministry as male priesthood. The second was in the emergence of the monarchical episcopate. These two developments led to an increased male dominance and therefore the submerging of women's participation in church leadership.

This is also evident in the next period of the history of the church, the Middle Ages. Life in the Middle Ages was characterized by deep religiosity and a deep desire to reform the church. Even though women were excluded from official roles in the church, such as the ecclesial hierarchy or scholastic theological scholarship, women played important parts in the life of the medieval church. In many ways these were destroyed through the Reformation.

In the early Middle Ages, abbesses like Hilda of Whitby or Etheldreda of Ely ruled over double monasteries of women and men, which were basically women's communities that needed men to administer the sacraments. Abbesses were highly educated and very powerful women. This is evident, for example, in St. Hilda's involvement in the Council of Whitby (664 CE).

Women were also involved in the deep search for God among the medieval mystics. Feminist theologians have devoted a large amount of their attention to the saints and mystics of the Middle Ages. Among them are women as diverse as Julian of Norwich, Mechthild of Magdeburg, Margery Kempe, Angela of Foligno, Catherine of Siena, Christine de Pisan, and Hildegard of Bingen. Mysticism enabled women to have religious experiences that were essentially beyond the control of male religious leaders. Again, none of them were feminists, and they all lived within structures that we would describe as patriarchal; but they are examples of a Christian spirituality that does, for example, use female imagery for the divine.

Much in the spiritual writings of medieval women is alien to readers in the twenty-first century. One example would be a eucharistic spirituality that aims to feed solely on the host and has severe starvation as a consequence. Its value for feminists today, however, lies in the fact that medieval women do appear as authors in their own right and demonstrate how women, long before the advent of feminism, made space for their own spirituality within a male-dominated church.

Medieval theology can therefore not be restricted to scholastics such as Thomas Aquinas and Albert the Great, but must take into account mystical authors such as Hildegard of Bingen and Catherine of Siena. Medieval women could not be theologians or members of the clergy. This, however, does not mean that some medieval women did not take authority within the church. For example, Catherine of Siena who in 1370 advised the pope to return to Rome was later made a doctor of the church. Hildegard chose to found her own convent in order to be independent from the leadership of the male monastery; she too advised the pope, the emperor, and bishops. By the thirteenth century women appear as authors of saints' lives and other kinds of devotional literature, often written for their fellow nuns or beguines.

Research on women in the Reformation has so far been scarce. It would therefore be easy to say that the Reformation, both on the European continent and in England, was a men's event that if anything got rid of the few recognized forms of women's presence in the established church. Such examples would be that of the opportunity of religious life and the veneration of Mary, the mother of Christ. Yet that does not mean that women were not involved in the Reformation. An example is Argula von Grumbach, the first Protestant woman to have her pamphlets distributed through the newly available printing press. Twenty-nine thousand of her pamphlets circulated around Germany at the time of the Peasants' War, which makes her one of the major authors of pamphlets in the age of the Reformation.

One of the ways the Reformation challenged the existing social order was in its renewed emphasis on the importance of the patriarchal family as a micro-cosmos within society and a domestic church. For women this meant to a large extent a restriction of their role. Women were limited to being housewives and mothers. Luther himself had after all argued that women would be redeemed through giving birth to children. In his search for a thorough reform of the church, Luther also advocated the importance of education. Luther mentions women's education in particular. Even though the Reformation created a number of potentially liberating features, such as the availability of Scripture in the vernacular and an emphasis on the priesthood of all believers, these remained largely in the hands of a male-dominated and clerical church.

While the Reformation itself did not see many women among its protagonists, with the notable exception of women such as Argula von Grumbach, the period after the Reformation was again one in which women were increasingly making spaces for themselves and their own spirituality. While officially recognized roles such such as the sacramental priesthood, preaching, and academic theology were not available to women, women again sought to make their own spaces by spiritual practices that have often been viewed with suspicion by the mainstream church. The most prominent among these are prophecy and mysticism. Examples of such women were the prophetesses among the radical Pietists or the French mystical writer Madame Guyon.

Of particular importance for feminist theologians are Quaker women. Quakerism has from its very beginnings argued for the equality of men and women with regard to every aspect of life, including Christian ministry. The Quakers have officially allowed women to participate in full-time ministry since the early 1800s. In fact, women had been involved in the Quaker movement from its earliest days.

Among the most prominent early Quaker women was Margaret Fell, who made her home Swarthmore Hall available as a base for the newly founded movement, and after the death of her husband Judge Fell devoted her whole life to the movement. She reminded King Charles II of his promise of religious tolerance within his kingdom and sought his help and support for the Quakers' rejection of military service and their refusal to swear any form of oath. Together with her second husband George Fox, the founder of the Quaker movement, Margaret Fell was imprisoned and threatened with the loss of her property. She persistently refused to give up preaching the Quaker faith and making her home available for Quaker meetings. Her daughters sought an audience with the king and ensured that Swarthmore Hall should not be given up. Margaret Fell and other early Quaker women argued for women's right to public preaching.

While the dissolution of the monasteries in sixteenth-century England was the end of one of the main opportunities for women to devote their lives to God and to gain status in the church, the Oxford movement in the nineteenth century enabled women to join newly founded religious communities in which women were able to live a life of prayer, community, and social work.

On a much wider scale, women within the established church were becoming involved in social concerns such as the struggle against the Contagious Diseases Act. This meant that women assumed roles that were much more public than the domestic role assigned to them by both the Reformers and Victorian Christianity. This increasing interest in public presence is epitomized in the struggle for women's suffrage by figures such as the Pankhurst sisters. Women were fighting to be admitted to vote both in ecclesial and in parliamentary elections — to be recognized as full lay members of the church and as full citizens of the state. Yet it was not until after the First World War that women actually gained the full right to vote.

The names mentioned here represent a selection of women who have gained prominence in the history of a church that has otherwise been dominated by men. Such a selection must be viewed critically as it is in danger of focusing on those women who assumed public roles, i.e., roles considered significant and notable by a church that is dominated by male clerical structures. Much more work on the history of women's lives in the church is needed. Yet feminist church historians must not focus exclusively on those women who have achieved a public role. In other words, feminist church historians must not focus on roles that have been noted by a male audience, but must take into account the presence of women in the church as worshipers and as readers of spiritual works that were to a large extent not written with their presence in mind.

The previous paragraphs have focused to a large extent on women in the church. Yet the other area in which women's presence needs to be noted and rethought is that of academic theology. Even though most theologians throughout the history of the Christian church until relatively recently have been men, a history of the developments prior to actual feminist theology has to mention those women whose work and presence has remained hidden.

A prominent example is Charlotte von Kirschbaum, Karl Barth's assistant and close companion in the writing of his seminal *Church Dogmatics.* Large parts of the *Church Dogmatics,* possibly the most influential work of Protestant theology in the twentieth century, were researched by Charlotte von Kirschbaum. Though she was never given the opportunity to study theology, von Kirschbaum devoted her whole life to the theology of her mentor and friend Karl Barth. Von Kirschbaum is buried in the Barth family grave. She died in a mental institution from the constant struggle of working with and for Karl Barth as his indispensable companion, all the while constantly denying her own femininity and thus destroying her personality. Von Kirschbaum's own works, which have only recently been published, identify her as a theologian in her own right, one who advocated the equality of women in the order of creation long before the advent of feminism. They are particularly interesting in the light of Barth's own views on the subordination of women as part of the order of creation.

None of the women mentioned in the first half of this chapter used the word "feminist" for their involvement in theological or faith discourses. Yet all of them are important as predecessors and foremothers who prepared the way for the development of feminist theology proper — to the development of which we now turn.

Even though we cannot speak about "feminist theology" as such until about the early 1970s, some earlier developments in the twentieth century are of particular significance. These show that feminist theology is always a discourse on the boundary between church and academia. Four factors are of particular importance for the development of feminist theology: the Second Vatican Council, the rise of liberation theologies, the movements for the ordination of women, and the feminist movement per se.

The starting point of feminist theology could be seen in Mary Daly's book *The Church and the Second Sex*. Later renounced by the author, who subsequently left Christianity, the book was a response to the situation of women in the Roman Catholic Church, which had not changed despite the transformations that resulted from the Second Vatican Council. Daly used Simone de Beauvoir's ideas and applied them to the history of women and the church. It is significant that most of the early feminist theologians were Roman Catholics. The main reason for this is that in spite of an all-male clergy, Roman Catholicism had actually preserved space for the significance of women. The Protestant churches of the Reformation had dissolved convents and abandoned the veneration of Mary and female saints. These, however, had remained in existence in the Roman Catholic Church and provided important, though highly ambivalent, starting points for Roman Catholic women. Roman Catholic women found themselves, on the one hand, in a church that had defined and acknowledged spaces for them, but on the other hand they were faced with an institution that rejected their ministry. Out of this ambivalence the women's movement in the Roman Catholic Church came into being.

Another important factor was the quest for the ordination of women. While a number of Protestant churches had begun to ordain women, Roman Catholic women were and are still faced with an all-male hierarchy. The latter excludes women from participation in the ordained priestly ministry and argues that to ordain women would be in contradiction to the order of creation and redemption. The experience of being excluded from the power centers of the church has been and still is a strong driving force for Roman Catholic women.

In 1976 and on several occasions since, the Vatican declared that, despite the fact that there were no theological objections to the ordination of women, it could not change its position and admit women to the sacramental priesthood. Pope John Paul II advocates a theology of the "dignity and vocation of women," which effectively reduces women to being mothers or nuns. While the movement for the ordination of women in the Roman Catholic Church still exists, other Roman Catholic women have decided against fighting for ordination in a church that is otherwise a male-dominated institution. To do so, they argue, would mean asking for a token gesture that effectively helps to sustain patriarchy rather than transform the church. This perceived stalemate led to the founding of the Women-Church movement.

The history of the women-church movement illustrates a variety of trends that also apply to the development of feminist theology in general. Feminist theology has become more diverse, in that it takes into account the different contexts in which women live. Feminist theology seeks to transcend the boundaries that restrict conventional patriarchal theology. These are, for example, the boundaries of an existing canon, the boundaries of church institutions and denominations, and the boundaries of Christianity itself. Feminist theology is to be in critical and constructive dialogue with other traditions of faith and those outside and on the margins of institutions ecclesial and academic.

In the Protestant churches, the development of feminist theology is closely connected with the "Women's Desk" of the World Council of Churches. From its beginning, women have played a significant part in the World Council of Churches. The first message from the Assembly of the WCC was written by a woman. This was unheard of in any form of church assembly. In one of its first meetings, Willem Visser 't Hooft, one of the founders of the WCC, argued that local churches could not expect to achieve renewal unless women were given more responsibility. The ecumenical movement provided a context in which women could and did form networks as they began to recognize many of the differences between denominations as artificial impositions of a male-dominated church that essentially hindered the unity of the body of Christ. The WCC not only provided a platform for women's cooperation across cultural and denominational boundaries, but also supported the dialogue between women and men in the church.

In 1954, the Department on the Cooperation of Men and Women in the Church was founded. Its purpose was to remind churches of the importance of cooperation between women and men as part of the churches' witness to the world. This found its most important expression in the 1981 Sheffield consultation, "The Community of Men and Women in the Church." The women of the WCC provided a platform for a diversity of backgrounds and concerns of women from all over the world. This gave, for example, African and Asian women a voice long before they came into their own right in the development of feminist theology.

The second half of the twentieth century saw the development of the women's movement, especially among white middle-class women in the United States. As a consequence, feminist theory and women's studies as an academic discipline were developed. The women's movement was triggered by a variety of social changes relevant to women in North American society. Among these was the increasing number of women in employment outside their homes. Other changes, such as the development and wider availability of contraceptives, transformations of traditional family structures (such as the rising divorce rate), and an increasing awareness of violence and discrimination against women were also involved. In addition, heterosexuality was no longer the only form of publicly recognized and accepted sexual identity and practice.

Feminist theory, then, analyses the situation of women in society and the factors that shape the lives and images of women. It seeks to develop a critical and transformative praxis that enables women's liberation. Feminist theology (though to a limited extent) draws on feminist theory as a resource for developing its own critical discourses, new narratives, and practices of faith.

While chapter 1 has outlined some of the general historical and methodological parameters within which feminist theologians seek to do Christian theology in a critical and constructive way, chapter 2 will look at how feminists have engaged with particular aspects of Christianity and responded to the challenges presented to them. It is to these that I now turn.

2. *Themes in Feminist Theology*

Scripture and the development of Christian thought through the two thousand years of Christian history provide the main resources for doing Christian theology. Feminist theologians understand doing theology to be a constructive process in critical dialogue with the Christian tradition. While the first chapter of this introduction has focused on Scripture and history, I will now move on to some of the constructive theological endeavors of feminist theologians. However, before we tackle some of the particular theological *loci,* some introduction to the terminologies and concepts used by feminist theologians is necessary.

Theology, Androcentrism, Sex, and Gender

Feminist theologians argue that sex, gender, bodies, and experience matter and are in fact important for doing theology. "Sex" describes the biological existence of human beings as men and women, while "gender" refers to the denotations made to each of these biological categories by culture and/or theology. These denotations affect not only the situation of each individual, male or female, but also all concepts of human relationships and power structures, in fact all aspects of both individual and corporate life.

Among the most prominent of these cultural connotations is the description of woman as *the Other,* the one who does not fit the male norm and therefore has to be secondary. Women are described as weak and feminine, as emotional and belonging to the realm of nature, while masculinity

25

and maleness are denoted with strength, rational thinking, and culture. Gender analysis is concerned with the origins and consequences of sexual identities and sexual differences, and with power structures and institutionalized relationships such as marriage or the clerical hierarchies of the church. Gendered concepts are prevalent in each and every aspect of life.

Feminist theology identifies traditional Christian theologies as inherently gendered and dualistic. In order to create a new and different way of doing theology, it is necessary to go further back and ask how the Christian tradition developed such an androcentric bias in the first place. A theologically based concept of gender difference has its origin in the use of dualistic Greek philosophical systems such as Platonism and Aristotelianism in medieval Christian theology. The creation accounts in the first book of the Hebrew scriptures could therefore be read in a way that suggests Adam was created first and Eve was derived out of Adam and therefore had to be secondary. Men were viewed as created directly in the image of God, while women were seen as being formed only indirectly in the image of God. Arguments like this helped create a male-female dualism similar to other dualistic constructions that counterbalance mind and body, rational and emotional, culture and nature, and even divine and human (while understanding the divine side to be male and the human side to be female). Genevieve Lloyd's monograph *This Man of Reason* provides a comprehensive account of the construction of dualism and gender difference in Western culture and philosophy. Some authors suggest that women had to become male in order to attain the fullness of salvation, as original sin had come upon humanity through the female. Sara Maitland describes "dualism" as a "heresy" that "means splitting the wholeness of God's creation into divisions labeled 'good' and 'bad.'"[1] Feminist theology, on the other hand, encourages a worldview that is capable of living with ambiguities and seeks to overcome the black-and-white view of the world.

The aim of feminist theology, however, is not a "gender-neutral" theology, but one that is aware of the existence of such gender bias and points out the contingency of gender constructions. This inherent gender bias is named *patriarchy*. The British feminist theologian Elizabeth Stuart describes patriarchy as:

---

1. Sara Maitland, *A Map of a New Country: Women and Christianity* (London: Routledge and Kegan Paul, 1983), p. 37.

... the name given to a web of systems which have developed in human history in which *some* male experience is made normative and most of the power to define and order reality is placed in the hands of men who are required to embody a particular construction of masculinity.[2]

Patriarchy constructs a social-symbolic order in which men dominate women and women are viewed as the Other: as those who do not fit the criteria of normative existence. Patriarchy is a system, a web of relationships and institutions that not only refers to relationships between men and women, but arranges the whole of life, and all forms of relationships, in a hierarchical way. Patriarchal interests within Christian theology and praxis have rendered women invisible in both church and theology. The exclusion of women from being church in a visible way is identified as *sexism*.

Elisabeth Schüssler Fiorenza prefers the term *kyriarchy* (i.e., "male-defined relationships of ruling") in order to describe "a socio-cultural, religious, and political system of elite male power, which does not just perpetrate the dehumanization of sexism, heterosexism, and gender-stereotypes but also engenders other structures of women's oppression, such as racism, poverty, colonialism, and religious exclusivism."[3] It is the task of women and feminist theologians in particular to create a counter-space to patriarchy or kyriarchy in which women may not only analyze and reflect on patriarchal oppression, but also find new and constructive ways of doing theology and reading the Bible.

Feminist theologians ask: Does the fact that women have been marginalized, silenced, and oppressed by the Christian churches throughout most of their history mean that Christianity as such is bad for women, or is it possible to write theology in a way that advocates the full humanity of women in the image of God? Is it possible to write a theology in which women are seen as those without whom the body of Christ is incomplete? Could the message of Christianity in fact be interpreted in a way that advocates women's experience and equality?

2. Elizabeth Stuart, *Just Good Friends: Towards a Lesbian and Gay Theology of Relationships* (London: Mowbray, 1995), p. 24.

3. Elisabeth Schüssler Fiorenza, "Introduction: Feminist Liberation Theology as Critical Sophialogy," in *The Power of Naming: A Concilium Reader in Feminist Liberation Theology* (London: SCM, 1996), p. xxi.

But what is women's experience and how is it different from men's experience? Is there any difference at all? And what are feminist theologians aiming for? Some feminist theologians argue for equal rights for women in the church. Through the indiscriminate admission to Christian baptism, women and men are considered equal in the church and therefore should be granted the same rights of participation. Yet the question that arises is: What are those equal rights and who defines what they are? Do equal rights for women, which are still based on the experiences and needs of men, provide an adequate basis for the lives of women in the church? Some feminists argue against a mythical understanding of the special nature of women, which perceives "anatomy as destiny" and accepts the physical differences between men and women as the basis for the exclusion of women from full participation in the church. Others argue that there are in fact differences between women and men that can be used in positive and constructive ways to define and redefine the church.

We therefore have to distinguish between two different groups of feminist theologians: those who aim to either find or create a theological base for women's equality, and those who propose to celebrate women's difference and women's identities as women. While the former are mainly found among North American liberal and liberation theologians, the latter are influenced by French psychoanalytical feminists such as Luce Irigaray and Julia Kristeva. Beyond these, a third group argues against the universal claims implicit in using the term "women" in a generic way without taking account of the differences among women themselves.

Feminist theology understands itself as an *advocacy theology*. Women are the subjects of theology, both in terms of being authors of theology and in terms of defining what is being studied. The agenda of feminist theology is one of justice and the full humanity of women. Feminist theology critically addresses patriarchal biases within theology and promotes awareness of the role played by Christian theology in condoning and advocating patriarchy. This awareness can then lead to developing a new way of doing theology that no longer accepts particular gender constructions as given, but works towards their transformation into theological concepts that enable and advocate a more inclusive and diverse theology and church.

The critical-praxis feminist theologians have provided a wealth of creative re-readings of all aspects of Christian theology. In this chapter I will give a number of examples of such critical, creative, and constructive re-

readings. Feminist theologians do not write "systematic theology" in the classical sense. Traditional theological systems are part of the patriarchal agenda, which feminist theologians not only evaluate critically but seek to replace by theological concepts that aim for liberation and transformation.

Beyond the Maleness of God: Rethinking Male God-Language

In the early 1970s, American feminist theologian Mary Daly stated provocatively: "If God is male, the male is God." Daly, and many other feminist theologians with her, sought to point out what consequences were implicit for Christian women in a theology that described God as a Father who begets a Son. Carol Christ argued: "To know ourselves as daughters of a Father God who claims to be the only parent is to be involved in a pathologically dependent relationship in which our strength and power as women can never be affirmed."[4] The exclusive use of masculine language and imagery for all three persons of the Trinity, however, limits the divine communion of persons to being an all-male nuclear family. This removes God from the lives and experiences of women and therefore renders much God-language meaningless for contemporary women. Feminist theologians understand their critique of exclusively male God-language as inseparable from a critical analysis of its use as a means of justifying and enforcing the marginalization, abuse, and oppression of women. It is against this background that Dorothee Sölle asks: "Can the word 'father' still mean 'God' when we have learned that God and liberation are mutually inclusive concepts?"[5] A feminist theological reconsideration of the divine has two aspects that are essentially intertwined: a critical analysis of the language and imagery used for the divine in the Christian tradition — and the effect this has on the experiences of women — and the development of new names and images for the divine that take into account the possibility of female names for God, and the understanding of God as the realization of those values, such as equality, mutuality, and affirming love, that are important to feminist theologians.

4. Carol P. Christ, *Laughter of Aphrodite: Reflections on a Journey to the Goddess* (San Francisco: Harper & Row, 1987), p. 93.
5. Dorothee Soelle in Fiorenza, *The Power of Naming*, p. 150.

The first step of this critique is to search the scriptures, and in fact the whole of the Christian tradition, for alternative ways of naming God. Julian of Norwich, for example, speaks of God as both father and mother; the Syriac liturgical tradition refers to the Holy Spirit as female. A number of feminist theologians, such as Elizabeth Johnson and Jann Aldrege-Clanton, have also explored the concepts of divine wisdom. Ideas of wisdom first appeared in a patriarchal context within a framework of androcentric thinking, but need to be read and constructively re-read within an egalitarian framework that releases their liberating potential. Canadian feminist theologian Janet Martin Soskice argues for the importance of "metaphors" in our reconsideration of "God-language" and imagery used for the divine. This means to rethink the implications of particular metaphors used for the divine, what they mean and what they do not mean. For example, does the notion of divine fatherhood evoke the idea of male dominance and therefore the subordination of women, or does it simply signify the relationship between the first and the second person of the Trinity? Feminist debates about God are critical of both language and imagery used in Christian theology and worship. They argue for a reinterpretation of traditional imagery, such as God as Father or God as wisdom, and for the creation of new imagery that does not restrict the divine to the confines of patriarchal theology.

While some feminist theologians solve the problems created by masculine God-language through replacing it with female names for the divine or extending the possible use of metaphors on the grounds that God is beyond the human concepts of sex and gender, others argue that a debate about the divine is only possible in the light of human embodiment and sexuality. Carter Heyward points out that it does not make much sense to understand God as being beyond sexuality and gender, but rather as immersed within our gendered and erotic particularities. She therefore suggests that one should ascribe a fluidity of gender to God that allows reference to God as "she" or "he" depending on personal needs.

The basic question for feminist theologians is: What does it mean to speak about God in the light of women's experiences of suffering and injustice, but also of love and joy? In the context of Christian theology this involves a critical reflection of the meaning of God as Trinity. Must the Trinity be perceived as an all-male divine club or is there scope for a re-reading of God as being in relation that also affirms relationships between women? Sallie McFague, in her search for metaphors of God that might be meaningful in the face of possible nuclear destruction, suggests seeing God as Mother, Lover, and Friend as well as Father, Son, and Holy Spirit. The focus, however, cannot be only on a possible renaming of individual persons of the Trinity, but on the divine as a whole.

There is precedent within the Christian tradition for understanding God as mother as well as father. Both Julian of Norwich and Anselm of Canterbury do so. Yet for feminist theologians, praying to God as mother entails a move beyond the use of parental imagery. It implies a search for an understanding of God that heals and affirms, that encompasses the experience of violence, alienation, and rejection, of negative understandings of the female body. Yet maternal imagery alone is not sufficient as its exclusive use would reduce women to their reproductive function and would exclude those women who, by choice or otherwise, are not mothers. Praying to God as "she" is a way of subverting male-dominated theology and exploring the breadth and multifacetedness of the divine. Such an exploration also includes an awareness of the limitations of any form of symbolic language. The use of paternal and parental imagery might be oppressive for those who themselves have suffered from painful experiences at the hands of their parents.

Central to feminist theological reflections on the nature of God is also the search for an embodied understanding of God. God is no longer "wholly other," but has to be found within the embodied realities of women's lives. Christian theology is essentially incarnational theology, which speaks of God as the one who took on a particular human body. Yet divine embodiment cannot be reduced to the incarnation alone. Some authors speak of God as mother giving birth to the world, others of God suffering in the suffering of humanity. Grace Jantzen and Sallie McFague also talk about the world as God's body. Embodiment is understood as identification with the human and the non-human creation that challenges human beings to celebrate their own lives as in the image of the divine.

According to Christian theology, God is both one and three. God's being is in relation. The divine Trinity is therefore not hierarchical, but a dynamic and life-giving relationship of three distinct persons. Our understanding of God as being in relation has to be essentially linked to the structuring of human relationships and communities. God is not an isolated ruling monarch, but a relational and dynamic mystery of love, as Elizabeth Johnson puts it in her book *She Who Is: The Mystery of God in Feminist Theological Discourse*. She argues for a feminist re-reading of the Christian doctrine of the divine Trinity:

31

The trinitarian symbol radically affirms the hope that God really is in accord with what has been mediated through experience, in other words, that Sophia-God corresponds to herself in bedrock fidelity. The thought to which it gives rise evokes a sense of ultimate reality highly consonant with the feminist values of mutuality, relation, equality and community in diversity.[6]

She summarizes her reclaiming of the Trinity from a feminist perspective as follows:

The trinitarian symbol intimates a community of equals, so core to the feminist vision of ultimate shalom. It points to patterns of differentiation that are non-hierarchical, and to forms of relating that do not involve dominance. It models the ideal, reflected in so many studies of women's ways of being in the world, of a relational bonding that enables the growth of persons as genuine subjects of history in and through the matrix of community, and the flourishing of community in and through the praxis of its members. In this vision personal uniqueness flourishes not at the expense of relationship but through the power of profound companionship that respects differences and values them equally: an aim mirrored in the symbol of the Trinity.[7]

God, understood in this way, symbolizes openness not only among persons divine or human, but essentially openness to the whole of creation. Such an understanding of the triune God, no longer a monolithic ruling monarch, but a loving communion of persons open to the world, is a prophetic voice against the patterns of dominance and oppression prevalent in this world.

Feminist theologians' reflections about God therefore take their starting point from what it means to be human. Human reality is created and shaped by particular conceptions of the divine. This connection between the human and the divine is most clearly seen in the fundamental Christian belief that the second person of the Trinity was both human and di-

6. Elizabeth Johnson, *She Who Is: The Mystery of God in Feminist Discourse* (London: SCM, 1993), p. 211.

7. Johnson, *She Who Is*, p. 219.

vine. It is to the Christian doctrine of Christology and the challenges it has created for feminist theologians that we now turn.

Challenging the Maleness of Christ: Feminist Approaches to Christology

The incarnation is at the heart of Christian belief about both the divine and the human: God, the wholly other, the eternal divine, makes Godself known by taking on humanity. Yet it has been precisely this act of making known the nature of the divine that has created a number of difficulties for feminist theologians. Not all feminist theologians identify with traditional Christianity in accepting the concept of the two natures of Christ and the importance of salvation through Christ. Yet at the same time, feminist theology that locates itself within the Christian tradition cannot avoid discussing the significance of Jesus the Christ for women's discourses of Christian faith. Jann Aldredge-Clanton argues that Christianity itself is at stake unless Christians manage to develop a Christology that "includes female, male, and all creation in new and empowering ways."[8]

One of the limitations of feminist christologies is that they focus almost exclusively on the human person of Jesus, whom Aldredge-Clanton portrays as a male whose ministry is open to women. Yet that in itself is a reduction of who Christ is, a male person in the most prominent position within the social-symbolic order of Christian theology. At the same time it is a critique of much traditional Christology, which focuses on the divinity of Christ and uses his maleness as a theological and political tool to oppress women and to perpetuate their abuse at the hands of men and male-dominated social and ecclesial structures.

Rosemary Radford Ruether, one of the earliest feminist theologians to ask the Christ-question, formulates it as follows: Can a male savior save women? Two issues are raised by this provocative way of putting it: What is the significance of the maleness of Christ and what is salvation? In other words: Who and what saves us and what do we need saving from?

The significance of the maleness of Christ has been one of the most central issues for feminist reconsiderations of Christology. Elizabeth A.

8. Jann Aldredge-Clanton, *In Search of the Christ-Sophia: An Inclusive Christology for Liberating Christians* (Mystic, Conn.: Twenty-Third Publications, 1995), p. 2.

Johnson identifies three areas in which the maleness of Christ is abused to the detriment of women within traditional Christianity:

1. Christ is seen as the revelation of God and therefore his maleness is understood as an essential characteristic of this revelation and therefore of the divine itself. If God is the Father, who has eternally begotten the Son, then the divine itself must be male, and members of the male sex must as a consequence be closer to the divine than members of the female sex.
2. Because Christ became incarnate as a male, men understand themselves as christomorphic because they bear physical resemblance to Christ. This argument is often used in the debate about the ordination of women to the ministerial priesthood: the priest who represents Christ to the congregation at the Eucharist does not resemble Christ in every way.
3. Traditional christological concepts are structured in a dualistic form that suggests the divine assumed male flesh. Only what has been assumed can be redeemed, which can be interpreted as female sexuality not having been assumed and therefore not redeemed in quite the same way as male sexuality.

Elizabeth Johnson argues that an anthropology based on a diversity of ways of being human provides the starting point for a Christology that is no longer focused on the maleness of Jesus in an ideologically distorted way.[9] The task is therefore to find ways of writing christologies that overcome a dualistically distorted anthropology, and in turn to use a fully human incarnation — rather than one that is only male — as the basis for affirming women's being in Christ. This does not necessarily mean that feminist theologians have to deny the particularity of Christ as a male human being. To be a sexual human being is an essential aspect of being fully human and therefore an essential aspect of the incarnation. However, what feminist theologians criticize is the ideological abuse of one particular aspect of the humanity of Jesus as theologically determinative of his identity or normative for the identity of the Christian community.

Christology in a feminist theological paradigm challenges an understanding of the incarnation and the life, death, and resurrection of Jesus

9. Johnson in Fiorenza, *The Power of Naming*, p. 311.

that is too spiritualized and ignores the realities of women's lives. As such it takes further the concept of Jesus Christ as liberator, developed by liberation theologians such as Leonardo Boff, and applies it to the particular situations of women. At the same time, feminist theologians realize that existing liberation christologies envisage Jesus as a hero of liberation who is beyond the vulnerability that is essential to being human. These christologies also do not take into account the realities of women's lives in the countries from which liberation theologies originate.

Rosemary Radford Ruether, in search of an answer to the question whether a male savior can save women, views the Jesus of the synoptic gospels as the prototype of liberated humanity. Jesus Christ can only be the liberator of women if we move beyond an individualistic concept of personal salvation to Christology as a theological discourse that challenges structural changes in church and society. This involves a close analytical reading of existing Christologies in order to dismantle them as tools of patriarchal abuses of power. Elisabeth Schüssler Fiorenza in her book *Jesus: Miriam's Child, Sophia's Prophet* engages in such a critical analysis and proposes the "*ekklesia* of wo/men" as the space where new and liberating ways of thinking about Jesus Christ can take place.

For authors such as Fiorenza and Elizabeth Johnson, this means a search of divine wisdom. Divine wisdom is a motive found throughout both the Hebrew and the Christian scriptures, and in her reconstruction of Christian origins Fiorenza seeks to show how sophialogy, the proclamation of Jesus as the prophet of divine wisdom and its personification, precedes any concept of Christology. She shows how the use of father/son language came to be used as a means of drawing boundaries for the early Christian communities and eliminating a cosmic element of thinking about Jesus that was perceived as too close to some of the surrounding religions of the Greco-Roman world. Johnson suggests retrieving the concept of Jesus-sophia in order to include female metaphors in our reflection on the divine process. She also uses it to illustrate the presence of everyday living in the life of the kingdom of God that Jesus proclaims. But most importantly, the idea of Jesus as sophia's prophet and personification affirms the fundamental openness of the divine to the whole of creation and to those who are excluded by existing structures of power and dominance: women, people of color, the poor, and the disabled.

One of the most controversial images of Christ is Edwina Sandys's statue of the crucified Christa, Christ represented as a woman, in the Cathedral St. John the Divine in New York. To portray Christ as a crucified woman is experienced by women as Christ identifying with their pain and thereby freeing them from the belief that, through being female and therefore guilty of original sin, they deserve to be raped or battered. Carter Heyward also uses the idea of the Christa, which moves away from focusing on the actual historical person of Christ. She speaks about the Christa as christic power in relation:

> Broken and deformed by abuse and fear, we are Christa: called/calling forth by the wild, compelling vision, or perhaps only the dim memory or faint hope, of one another's real presence in history, in time/space, in our lives as persons in relation. By the grace of this christic power in relation, we risk participating in our own creation/liberation. In so doing, though battered and bruised, we may form with one another, from a christian perspective, the soulful, sensual body of Christa — which is a sacred/christic movement of *compañeras,* a holy communion of friends, a spirited resource of hope for the earth and for its many and varied creatures.[10]

Heyward understands Christa as an embodied energy that, if released in us, will change the world. A collection of essays that represent the connection made between the death of Christ and the sexual abuse of women and children is found in the volume *Christianity, Patriarchy and Abuse.* Battered wives have often been encouraged by the priest from whom they sought help to endure as Christ had endured suffering at the hands of the Father on the cross. Some feminist authors have therefore moved away from the person of Christ as a male human being and focused more on the relationships of power transformed into love that are realized through the community of Christ.

The christological question has clearly been one of most powerful obstacles for feminist theologians in their engagement with and reconsideration of traditional Christian theology. Very few feminist theologians stick to traditional orthodox Chalcedonian Christology. In connection with the question of what it means for women that Christ was both divine and hu-

10. Carter Heyward, *Touching Our Strength: The Erotic as Power and the Love of God* (San Francisco: Harper & Row, 1989), p. 92.

man (male), three further areas have to be considered: what it means, from a feminist theological perspective, to be human; the question of sin and salvation (in other words: Is salvation necessary and salvation from what?); and finally, the question of female participation in salvation — the significance of Mary, the mother of Jesus Christ.

Feminist Theological Anthropologies and Women's Bodies

Theological anthropology is theological reflection on what it means to be human in the light of humanity's creation in the image of God, but also in the light of the fall of humanity. As already mentioned, feminist theological discussions about anthropology are closely connected with christological reflections, but the debate is wider and more fundamental: what it means to be human for women is at the very heart of feminist theological reconsiderations of theology.

Feminist theologians criticize most traditional Christian anthropology as focusing on men and male bodies, which are regarded as normative, while women are denied their voice in defining what it means to be human. Rosemary Radford Ruether distinguishes between one-nature and two-nature anthropologies. Anthropology that focuses on one human nature in the image of God is inevitably androcentric. It views woman as "the Other," the one who is deviant from normative humanity and therefore has less capacity for salvation. A two-nature anthropology is based on a concept of gender complementarity that understands sexual difference in terms of one sex not being complete without the other. Feminist anthropology seeks to develop a concept of community and humanity that is based on relationships of mutuality, reciprocity, and diversity. The fullness of being human is part of the original creation.

Two aspects are important to feminist theological reflections of being human: the significance of women's bodies and the idea of being human in relation. Women's bodies have throughout the Christian tradition been subject to denial. They have been regarded as ritually unclean and therefore in need of purification. Women's bodies and women's blood, shed in menstruation and childbirth, have been — and at times still are — considered as polluting and defiling anything and anybody coming in contact with them. Women have therefore been banned from the sanctuary (and still are, for example, in the Orthodox churches, advised not to take communion during menstruation).

In the modern world, women are subjected to ideals of what a woman's body should look like, imposed on them by the advertising industry and enforced through slimming programs that often use religious language to carry out their objectives ("sinning," "confessions"). Women are therefore made to feel uncomfortable in their own bodies and to work towards shaping them in an image that the male-dominated advertising industry has designed for them. This means that women are again reduced to being the object of male desire. Women have often been regarded as more closely connected with their bodies, their "biology being their destiny." Men on the other hand have been considered more rational and essentially overcoming the weakness of their bodies. And yet, a woman's body was instrumental in the most central act of the history of redemption, the incarnation. Feminist theologians argue that a Christian theology affirming the full humanity of women and the essential goodness of all creation needs to affirm and celebrate women and their bodies.

A first step towards such a celebration of women's bodies as part of the goodness of creation — as well as the reality of the sinfulness and fallenness of the world — is to take the reality of women's bodies seriously. Aspects of women's bodily lives, such as menstruation, are often treated with benign embarrassment or regarded as a curse that women have to bear as "daughters of Eve," who was responsible for the fall of humanity. The only way women are supposed to overcome their essential sinfulness is by either following a sacrificial concept of Christian motherhood that ensures redemption through childbirth, or by abstaining from their own sexuality in order to limit the effects of their own impurity on themselves and others. It is necessary for feminist theologians to reconsider the effects of such a teaching of sin and redemption on the reality of women's lives: "Women's experience is not only important but central in the creation of theology. This experience is sited in the body which includes the mind."[11]

Feminist theologians aim for a sacramental theology of women's bodies. Women's bodies can no longer be seen as polluting, as the objects of male desire, but as bodies that embody the body of Christ in many differ-

---

11. Lisa Isherwood and Elizabeth Stuart, *Introducing Body Theology* (Sheffield: Sheffield Academic Press, 1998), p. 10.

ent ways. Such a sacramental theology of the body affirms the goodness of creation and enables a truly incarnational theology.

Christian theology defines being human as being in relation to others and to God. Feminist theologians are critical of the restrictions that traditional theology has put on its understanding of which relationships are regarded as important and which are not. In most conventional theological thinking, women's being is defined through their relationships with men. Heterosexual marriage, or a form of celibacy that is reduced to being the absence of a heterosexual relationship, is understood as the normative relationship. Women are defined as not-men, as the second in creation.

One example is Karl Barth's theology of creation, in which he challenges women to accept that "men are A in creation while women are B" and denounces all other forms of sexual relationships as "unnatural and against the order of creation." The relationship between the male Christ, the head of the church, and his feminine submissive bride, the church, has been understood as the fundamental structure of the universe and the normative relationship that sets the norm for all other permissible relationships. This has been painful and life-denying to all those who do not feel called to live in a relationship with a member of the opposite sex or find their most meaningful relationships with members of their own sex.

Most early feminist theologians restricted their anthropological reflections to polarizing "male" and "female" and did not take into account the importance of a wide variety of different relationships, sexual and non-sexual, as meaningful for women. A sacramental and incarnational theology of women's bodies opens up the "canon" of relationships and affirms women's lives and women's bodies in relation as celebrations of the incarnation in this world.

Overcoming their female bodies, denying their female sexuality, and "becoming male" have in the past been perceived as the only ways for women to overcome their inherently sinful and polluting nature. Therefore a discussion of what it means to be human in a feminist theological paradigm evolves towards a reconsideration of the concepts of salvation and redemption.

Feminist Discourses of Sin and Salvation

One of the earliest debates in the context of feminist reinterpretations of symbols and theological concepts was the debate about the conception of sin and redemption in the light of women's experience. Sin has been associated with women through much of the Christian tradition, a concept that also helped to justify the necessity of a male savior. On the other hand, salvation, if at all possible for women, has been perceived as women achieving a form of spiritual masculinity that brings them closer to the male God than they could ever achieve as women. Feminist theologians such as Valerie Saiving and Judith Plaskow (in her doctoral dissertation *Sex, Sin and Grace*) have argued that traditional theological discourses about sin have no relevance for women, as they do not take account of the experiences of women. Feminist theologians argue that Christianity has helped to sustain the subordinate role attributed to women through this association with original sin and women's secondary position in creation.[12]

We can distinguish three different concepts of sin used by feminist theologians. Some feminist theologians seek to develop a concept of sin that takes account of sexual difference (even if such sexual difference is only created by Christian theology in the first place) and does not impose a concept of sin defined as pride, self-centeredness, and *hybris* on women. Women's sin could rather be defined as doing the exact opposite: in undervaluing themselves — not, in other words, developing a sense of self: a false self-denial.

Another dimension of this analysis of traditional concepts of sin is Mary Daly's understanding of sin as alienation from female being and female identity. Daly understands the biblical story of the fall of humanity as a patriarchal myth used to justify the oppression and marginalization of women. Women have sinned by internalizing the connection made between women and sin and by denying their own self-consciousness as women. Women therefore have to liberate themselves from male oppression and come into their own new being as women.

The third concept is the idea of sin being inherent in the structures of society. The most important and most damaging of these is sexism or pa-

12. Judith Plaskow, *Sex, Sin and Grace: Women's Experiences in the Theologies of Reinhold Niebuhr and Paul Tillich* (Washington, D.C.: University of America Press, 1980).

triarchy, the complex web of oppression not only of women, but of all aspects of creation rendered inferior. Feminist theologians seek to redefine sin as no longer the defilement brought into the world by women, but as those structures that sustain the domination of men over women. Rosemary Radford Ruether writes:

> Far from reflecting the true will of God and the nature of women, such theological constructions subvert God's creation and distort human nature. Feminist theology is about the deconstruction of these ideological justifications of male domination and the vindication of women's equality as the true will of God, human nature and Christ's redemptive intention.[13]

Feminist theology no longer holds a privatized or individual concept of salvation, but one that always takes place in the public arena. Salvation is no longer understood as personal redemption from sin (through substitutionary atonement), but as a vision of liberation, flourishing, and well-being for everyone. This inseparability of salvation as something that affects not only the individual human being, but society as a whole, is expressed in the feminist slogan: "The personal is the political." Feminist theologians regard a commitment to transformation and social justice as inseparable from doing theology and essentially as the criterion for the validity of all theological concepts.

The roots for the connection between women and sin lie in the story of the Fall in the book of Genesis. This story can be used as a justification for male domination over both women and the non-human creation. Anne Primavesi points out the inherent danger of such a reading of Genesis:

> This account has placed man above woman and Nature and legitimated this supremacy in the name of God. It has presented man's sexual relationship with woman as essentially one of domination. It has taught that work is a curse and hardship, and that raw matter is to be subdued into shape rather than related to as an object of con-

---

13. Rosemary Radford Ruether, *Women and Redemption: A Theological History* (London: SCM, 1998), p. 8.

templation. It has separated the area of transcendence, the sacred, from that of immanence, the earthly here and now.[14]

This leads to a new definition of redemption or salvation. Salvation is no longer the cleansing of the sinful human nature or reconciliation with an angry God, but the affirmation and reclamation of the original goodness of all human beings. Such redemption is centered on the human being and not on God. It creates good and healing relationships among human beings and between the human and the non-human creation.

Rethinking Mary and the Saints

Closely connected with feminist discourses on Christ, on being human, and on sin are feminist discussions on the possibility of reclaiming Mary, the mother of Christ. Feminist theologians face the challenge of a wide variety of traditions regarding Mary. Some of these have been detrimental for women, but women have also developed forms of Marian spirituality that are empowering and help to balance a male-dominated Christology. Mary has indeed been an ambivalent character for women. Because Mary is seen as both virgin and mother, a theology constructed by celibate male clergy has turned her into the ideal pure woman who is unlike other women. While women and their bodies, following the curse of Eve, are defiled through menstruation and childbirth, Mary is pure. At the same time, she is also humble. This has been used as an argument against the ordination of women to the ordained ministry: not even Mary, the highest and most spiritual female human being, the one closest to Christ, asked to be ordained, but submitted to the priesthood of her son. Traditional Marian theology can therefore be seen as an expression of men's inability to cope with women in positions of (ecclesial) power, but ultimately with women's bodies and their sexuality.

Rosemary Radford Ruether, in her book *Mary — The Feminine Face of the Church*, was one of the first feminist theologians to discuss a feminist approach to Mary. Ruether argues that Mary as the feminine personification of the church also represents the prototype of liberated humanity.

---

14. Anne Primavesi, *From Apocalypse to Genesis: Ecology, Feminism and Christianity* (London: Burns & Oates, 1991), pp. 63f.

Some feminist theologians understand Mary's virginity as a symbol of her independent choice to participate in God's work of salvation. Others see her as the important feminine side in a theology dominated by a male father-God.

Women in the Third World and in Latin America in particular have reinterpreted Mary as a symbol of liberation. Such a reinterpretation is based on the song of Mary, the Magnificat. In it, Mary praises God for his preferential option for the poor and the oppressed and thereby becomes the prophet of a new revolutionary spirituality of the people of God. For both Latin American and Asian women, Mary is present and empathizes with their daily struggles as mothers of children who suffer and are victims of oppressive, patriarchal regimes. For a feminist interpretation of Mary, it is vital to connect Mary with the daily lives and experiences of women rather than leave her in the realm of unattainable dogmas like the Immaculate Conception and the Assumption of Mary as Queen of Heaven.

Elisabeth Schüssler Fiorenza argues for a deconstruction of patriarchal Mariology and the symbolism involved. For her this means essentially the rejection of *all* patriarchal conceptions of both masculinity and femininity. On the other hand, the significant role Marian spirituality has in fact played for women compels feminist theologians to see Mary as an important symbol that has been claimed and reclaimed by women as a vital female figure in Christian theological symbolism. Mary is after all a woman who affirms the inevitable presence of women in the church. As a number of feminist theological discussions have shown (for instance, Els Maeckhelberghe's *Desperately Seeking Mary*), it is possible to apply a method of deconstruction and re-reading to Marian symbolism in order not to discard what is after all a vital symbol for women.[15]

Several feminist theologians (Elizabeth A. Johnson and Elizabeth Stuart in particular) have also argued for a feminist reappropriation of the concept of the communion of saints and the idea of saints as role models and companions on women's spiritual journeys. While feminist theologians are inevitably suspicious of the concept of the canonization of saints by the patriarchal church and by some of the role models found in the lives

---

15. See, for example, Els Maeckelberghe, "'Mary': Maternal Friend or Virgin Mother," *Concilium* 206 (1989): 120-27, and Catharina Halkes, "Mary and Women," *Concilium* 168 (1983): 66-73.

of saints that are detrimental for women, the concept of the communion of saints also points to a wide diversity of ways to live a Christian life and follow Christ that affirms women's presence throughout the history of the church.

To recover the concept of saints by finding models of faith, both historical and present, is therefore an important step towards rethinking the church itself as a place where women, their discourses of faith, and presence throughout the history of the church are represented and celebrated. Saints, in Elizabeth Stuart's view, are sources of encouragement and essentially friends for women rather than role models who represent unattainable ideals of a pure and holy life. The body of Christ is embodied through a multitude of saints past and present who tell, embody, and perform the story of Christ through their lives. The lives of saints are therefore not so much to be thought of as role models for women to imitate, but as a challenge to which women respond through their own discourses of faith and their reflections of what it means to be church. It is to feminist discourses of being church that we now turn.

"Women Are Church": Feminist Reconstructions of Ecclesiology

Similar to Scripture, the church as the key institution within Christianity has provided women with a situation of fundamental ambiguity: while women have on the basis of gender often been excluded from the power centers of the church, such as preaching or sacramental celebration, the majority of those who attend church services have traditionally been women. Yet for a number of feminist theologians this ambiguity has not so much triggered the choice of either staying within the existing structures of the church or leaving them behind altogether, but rather has challenged them to develop alternative visions of being church that function as empowerment for the transformation of existing structures.

Women's struggle for equal rights in the church has found its focal point in the debate about the ordination of women to the ministerial priesthood. In 1982, at a conference of the Center for Concern, a North American civil rights organization, Elisabeth Schüssler Fiorenza coined the phrase "Women are Church and have always been Church." This can be seen as the first beginnings of what later became the Women-Church movement. Fiorenza argued that even though there had been numerous councils throughout the history of the church, none of them had actually represented the full *ekklesia,* as women had always been denied access and representation by them. The *ekklesia* is the assembly or congress of those who have full citizenship and the right to vote.

Women-church is a movement of "self-identified women and women-identified men" that argues the patriarchal church can no longer claim to be the sole representation of being church and that the church cannot be church in its fullness until women are fully incorporated into it and fully participate in its decision-making. In 1983, a conference took place in Chicago, entitled "From Generation to Generation: Women-Church Speaks." Those participating understood the conference as the first occasion in history in which women publicly and collectively claimed to be church and sought publicly recognized participation and dialogue with the official church as well as attention to their concerns and issues.

Women-church did not seek to found a new organization or institution, but understood itself as a loose network of different groups and organizations affirming such values as equal rights, social justice, and mutuality. The ordination of women remains one of the many concerns represented by members of the movement, but can no longer be seen as the only one. Women's claiming to be church not only refers to struggling for admission to the existing hierarchy (or even its lowest ranks), but the transformation of the church as such. Liturgy and ritual are among the expressions of women-church, but it does not understand itself as an exclusively religious movement. For women-church, being church rather means political praxis and the struggle against violence, racism, sexism, and heterosexism.

Two further national conferences of the women-church movement took place in 1987 in Cincinnati and in 1993 in Albuquerque. Women-church continues to exist in the form of the "Women-Church Convergence," a network of organizations that meets once a year to discuss common concerns.

Women-church understands itself as a movement based on the concept of ecclesial communities in Latin American liberation theology. The development towards women-church can be described in three steps: women move from "impacting the church" through "identifying as church" to "proclaiming women-church" through the praxis of feminist liturgical base communities and civil rights organizations.

45

While Elisabeth Schüssler Fiorenza developed the original concept of women-church, Rosemary Radford Ruether reflected theologically on some of the practical implications in creative dialogue with feminist liturgical communities and women's experience of being marginalized within the church. Ruether identifies three areas in which women have been marginalized in the church. These are sacramental celebration, theological education, and ecclesial administration. These three areas need to be reappropriated to the people of the church and to women in particular. Ruether understands feminist liturgical base communities as "liberated zones" within the patriarchal church. They develop from the variety of needs of those who participate in them and have a critical function within the church while remaining outside the control mechanisms of its power structures. Feminist base communities for Ruether are parallel structures on the edge of the mainstream church that ensure the spiritual survival of women within the patriarchal structures of the church.

In order to create such liberated zones, women may have to withdraw temporarily from the male-dominated spaces of the church in order to develop their own forms and expressions of spirituality. Yet such separation is only meant to be temporary as the aim of women-church is the church as a liberated cohumanity of women and men. Ruether understands women-church as the *exodus* community that leads the church in its *exodus* from patriarchy. Mary E. Hunt understands the choice between conformity and separation as an expression of patriarchy itself, which no longer has meaning for women being church. Women-church rather represents a conscious ambiguity with regard to the structures, rituals, and symbols of the established church.

One of the ways in which patriarchy manifests itself within the church is "clericalism." "Clericalism" is a system that attributes all power of sacramental celebration, theological knowledge, and decision-making to experts, in other words: to members of the clergy on whom such power has been imparted through ordination. Women, on the grounds of their sex, are often excluded from such power. Clericalism creates divisions and hierarchical structures that are contrary to the feminist goals of liberation and equality. So, the "dismantling of clericalism" is one of the primary goals of a feminist transformation of the church. The existing clerical structures are to be replaced by models of ministry that empower and encourage the use of the gifts of all believers.

While most of the feminist debates about feminist reconstructions or reconceptualizations of the church have taken place in a Roman Catholic context, some feminist theologians from Protestant backgrounds have also reflected on the possibility of a feminist reconstruction of ecclesiology. The Presbyterian minister Letty Russell proposes a "round-table ecclesiology" that embodies a feminist spirituality of connection. Russell is indebted to liberation theology as a theological paradigm that takes its starting point from the experience of ecclesial praxis and advocacy of those on the margins of society and the church. Feminist ecclesiology for Russell is a feminist reevaluation of all aspects of the life of the church. She asks:

> How can we develop a feminist theory about the church that makes sense of women's reality and experiences of oppression and yet continues to affirm Jesus Christ as the source of life and connection of the Christian community?[16]

The church for Russell is the "community of Christ where everyone is welcome." The life and ministry of Christ is one that is open to all, and to those on the margins of society (including women); it is the focal point and the ultimate criterion of all ecclesial praxis. In practicing openness and hospitality to strangers, the church participates in and continues God's mission. Russell describes the church as a "round-table community" where everyone is welcome. She argues for the abolition of all clerical and hierarchical structures in the church in order to replace them with concepts of ministry that regard all ministries as of equal value. Leadership within the Christian community is necessary, but needs to be perceived as service that responds to the needs of the particular community. Russell's "round-table ecclesiology" is an open ecclesiology. Open, as it does not see itself as the only place where God is present and where salvation is possible, and also open in the sense that its structures are always provisional and constantly being reassessed. An open ecclesiology is also radically open to the future of God's kingdom and essentially open to the world and its needs. The church is the bearer of the prophetic tradition that criticizes patriarchy and announces liberation for all humanity. In doing that, it anticipates God's New Creation. Russell suggests that "justice" should be un-

---

16. Letty M. Russell, *Church in the Round: Feminist Interpretation of the Church* (Louisville: Westminster/John Knox, 1993), p. 21.

derstood as a fifth mark of the church (along with unity, holiness, catholicity, and apostolicity).

Feminist ecclesiology means a transformation, a re-framing of ecclesiological discourse. It also means rethinking all aspects of the life of the church. Two of these are of particular importance: the search for a feminist liberating spirituality and the church as a community of justice.

In her book *The Church in the Round,* Letty Russell argues for a feminist spirituality of connection and choice. Choice for her means the active choice to be a woman and to understand being a woman, having a woman's body as a celebration of being in the image of God rather than despised and rejected by patriarchy. Rosemary Radford Ruether in the second half of her book *Women-Church* suggests a number of feminist rituals. These new liturgies draw not merely on the Christian tradition, but also on the Jewish festivals and other non-Christian forms of spirituality that are affirming of women. They include rituals for the major stages in a woman's life such as menarche and menopause, liturgies of exorcism of patriarchal texts in the Bible (such as the rape of Dinah), and rituals for specific experiences such as a woman who has experienced rape, or a ritual after a divorce in which both partners are released from their vows and affirm their continuing responsibility and commitment for their children. A number of feminist communities have dedicated their work to the creation of women's spirituality. Among them are WATER (Women's Alliance for Theology, Ethics, and Ritual) and the St. Hilda's Community in London.

The theme of "justice" is closely linked with that of a feminist spirituality as women's spiritualities are deeply rooted in women's lives and the experience of women's lives has often been and still is one of fundamental injustice. Within the Women-Church Convergence there are therefore not only groups that in one way or another celebrate women's liturgies, but also groups that are dedicated to social justice with regard to issues of women's equal opportunities and women's choices of life and sexual orientation. Justice has to be redefined from a feminist perspective because traditional concepts of justice and equality have been based on the idea of a generic male human being rather than on the idea of right relationships. Right relationships can only be achieved if oppression and the abuse of power are named as such. Feminists see injustice based on sexism that in turn is part of the oppressive web of patriarchy. Other forms of oppression are exploitation, marginalization, powerlessness, cultural imperialism, and systemic violence. In arguing that justice should be the fifth mark of the church, Letty Russell suggests that the church cannot be the church if it does not fight for justice for those who are oppressed and on the margin. Justice from a feminist perspective means power-in-relation. Feminists advocate an epistemological privilege of those who are on the margin. Those who are silenced by oppression need to be given a voice to speak out for their concerns. Yet being given a voice is not enough. The struggle for justice must result in a transformation of the situation, in other words: in social change. To struggle as feminists for justice means to take action to transform concrete and particular relationships and situations. Therefore, justice cannot be a general concept, but has to take different forms in different contexts. Ada María Isasi-Díaz understands justice as a "theological-ethical praxis-reflective action geared to radical change at both the personal and societal level."[17] These two levels, says Isasi-Díaz, cannot be separated. Justice therefore connects both personal spirituality and being church for feminist theologians. The church becomes the visible sign of God's justice and proclaims the justice of God for all through its very being. Feminist theologians struggle not only for justice for women within the church, but also in all other aspects of life as feminists refuse to be restricted to man-made institutional boundaries.

Last Things or First? Feminists Questioning Eschatology

Feminist theology sees itself as rethinking the traditional methods and contents of theology. This also means reclaiming the power to define what is the subject of theology from the perspectives of the lives of women in past and present. What this means can be seen from the transformation of the theological *locus* of "the last things" or eschatology. Feminist theologians have so far not taken much interest in the study of the possibility of a future world, but rather in the healing and transformation/liberation of the present world. One of the expressions of this interest is in rethinking theology as not only referring to human beings, but to the whole of creation.

Ecofeminist theologians such as Rosemary Radford Ruether have drawn parallels between the destruction of the earth and the present ecological crisis and the oppression of women by men. The roots of the alien-

17. Isasi-Díaz, "Justice and Social Change," in *Dictionary of Feminist Theologies*, ed. Letty Russell and J. Shannon Clarkson (Louisville: Westminster/John Knox, 1996), p. 159.

ation between mind and body, between nature and culture, lie in sexism. Judeo-Christian theology has generated such alienation through a human-centered and essentially male-centered view of creation as the basis of a patriarchal religion and culture. Ruether proposes a new cosmology based on subatomic physics and evolutionary biology that overcomes the dualistic structures on which traditional Judeo-Christian concepts are based. This means discovering the interconnectedness of the whole of creation, human and non-human. Part of this process and essentially its core component is the reintegration of male and female in human society. Theologically this means a reintegration of *Gaia,* the earth-mother, and God.

Ecofeminist theology seeks to identify those tendencies in both Christian and Jewish theologies that sacralize the domination and negation of bodies, the earth, and women, and to find ways of affirming the goodness of all creation. This includes the development of concepts of redemption that are no longer dualistic. This is partly achieved through dialogue between different traditions of spirituality, but often results in an uncritical acceptance of non-Western concepts. Ruether suggests a spirituality that integrates covenantal and sacramental aspects with each other:

> In the covenantal tradition we find the basis for a moral relation to nature and to one another that mandates patterns of right relation, enshrining these right relations in law as the final guarantee against abuse. In the sacramental tradition we find the heart, the ecstatic experience of I and Thou, of interpersonal communion, without which moral relationships grow heartless and spiritless.[18]

Ruether proposes a concept of a God who is the personal center of the whole cosmic process "which all the small centers of personified being manifest and express."[19]

The constructive theme that follows from the ecofeminist critical analysis of patriarchy is that of the interconnectedness of all things. I have already mentioned Carter Heyward's concept of God as mutual relation. Mary Grey proposes an understanding of redemption as making right relationships. Catherine Keller understands God as the source of connected-

18. Rosemary Radford Ruether, "Theological Resources for Earth-Healing," *Feminist Theology* 2 (January 1993): 86.

19. Ruether, "Theological Resources for Earth-Healing," p. 97.

ness. She sees separation between persons and between human and non-human subjects as the fundamental shape of Western culture and as essentially connected with sexism.

The concept of "interconnectedness" suggests a perspective for doing theology that includes the whole of creation. Interconnectedness can be understood as an "epiphany of divine communication." Interconnectedness, however, cannot remain a romanticizing myth about relationships between humanity and nature, but must be seen with the challenges it proposes for a new feminist ethics of connections in mind. It is the Holy Spirit who overcomes dualistic structures and makes true connectedness possible. This is not only a model for the relationship between human and non-human creation, but also the basis for a new feminist ecclesiology of being connected through the Spirit as the energy of connection. Mary Grey argues for taking into account the ecological dimension in the reconsideration of ecclesiology: "Being Church is being with the rhythms of creation, sharing its travail, and acting for its well-being."[20] Catherine Keller contrasts the patriarchal self which is formed by separation and alienation with feminism which affirms the connectedness of the self.

Feminist theologians argue that Christian eschatology can no longer afford to be merely concerned with a transcendental world, but has to focus on the development of peace, justice, and right relationships in this world. Justice and connectedness are also central themes in feminist theological ethics.

Towards a Feminist Theological Ethic

Like any other feminist theological discourse, feminist theological ethics takes its starting point from a critical analysis of the ethical and moral concepts prevalent in traditional Christianity. What informs the basic paradigms behind them and how do they inform the moral choices made by women and the whole of women's lives? Beverly Wildung Harrison suggests that such a critical reevaluation has to start with a critical analysis of the moral effects of language and the way it constructs sexual differences and enforces just or unjust social relations. Traditional ethical concepts are

---

20. Mary Grey, *The Wisdom of Fools: Seeking Revelation for Today* (London: SPCK, 1993), p. 130.

not to be criticized for their neglect of femininity, but rather for their failure to take into account the concrete experiences of actual women. "We must lose no opportunity to challenge the pervasive, if subtle, implication that what pertains to women concretely or to women's culture is of lesser value than male norms or is a lesser expression of the best reality of the human species."[21] Harrison describes the goal of feminist liberation ethics as the full and concrete emancipation of women in all societies. This requires a process of constructively reasoning together.

Feminist theology is geared towards transformation and change both in individual lives and in the life of society. This transformation and change can only occur if feminist theology retains its commitment to social justice. The transformation of ethics into a discipline relevant to women's lives is therefore a result of the transformation of theology. Mary Grey proposes a feminist ethic that contrasts the tendencies of individualism and alienation within modern society with a model of connection, interdependence, and interconnectedness. Such a feminist ethic of connection and connectedness does not seek to romanticize human relationships, but draws attention to the connectedness and interdependence of the whole of creation.

Feminist ethical decision-making takes women's lives as its starting point. Human life must be regarded as embodied and therefore beyond a dualistic separation of body and mind. Feminist theological ethics challenges women to take responsibility for all aspects of their own lives "without hiding behind unquestioned assumptions about women's nature or women's traditional roles."[22] A feminist theological ethics seeks to reconsider those issues most relevant to the lives of women, such as abortion, reproductive rights and technologies, contraception, genetic engineering, and the value of women's work in the light of women's experiences. It implies a feminist critique of male control over nature and over women's lives. Women's experiences are regarded as a central resource for decision-making in a feminist paradigm of theological ethics.

It is important to bear in mind that women's experiences are very diverse and are informed by a wide variety of different factors such as class, race, or socio-economic situation. Attention to differences between

21. Beverly Wildung Harrison, *Making the Connections: Essays in Feminist Social Ethics,* ed. Carol S. Robb (Boston: Beacon, 1985), p. 31.

22. Linda Hogan, "Ethical Theory," in *An A-Z of Feminist Theology,* ed. Lisa Isherwood and Dorothea McEwan (Sheffield: Sheffield Academic Press, 1996), p. 57.

women's lives as well as sexual difference together with the significance of the particularity of different situations are a vital basis for the development of a theological ethics informed by feminist theology.

One of the central ethical questions arising from the lives of many women is that of the nature, value, and significance of women's work. How can women integrate work and motherhood? "How might theological doctrines of love, self-sacrifice, creation, procreation, vocation and community better respond to women and men who want to work in fulfilling ways and love in intimate relationships, including those that involve raising children?"[23]

Feminist theological ethics takes a critical approach to the values traditionally used in ethical decision-making and evaluates their significance for women and their effect on women's lives. Women's experiences and praxis are primary factors in developing an ethics that advocates justice for women and embodies the values advocated by feminist theology as a whole. It also seeks to introduce and advocate a new range of values focusing on what is relevant for the development of women's lives in just relationships. Feminist theological ethics cannot be isolated from other aspects of theological discourse, as all feminist theological reflections have an ethical dimension: feminist theology understands itself as advocating change and transforming structures of injustice into right relationships.

Feminist Theologies from Different Contexts

Since about the mid-1980s, feminist theology has become increasingly diverse. Hispanic and black women were among the first to identify the feminist theologians they encountered as claiming to speak for all women without taking into account the diversity of women's experiences. The earliest feminist theologians came from a predominantly white, middle-class, educated North American background that did not resemble the experiences of black or Hispanic women. Among the most important movements that developed through this process of diversification were Hispanic or *mujerista* theology, Black or *womanist* theology, and feminist theology in a European context.

23. Bonnie J. Miller-McLemore, *Also a Mother: Work and Family as Theological Dilemma* (Nashville: Abingdon, 1994), p. 23.

Womanist theologians are feminists of color who attempt to speak of God in the context of the experiences of African American women. The white feminist theologian Susan Brooks Thistlethwaite understands the differences between the experiences of black and white women as the starting point for doing theology. She argues that such differences are to be respected. This involves avoiding the universalization of the experiences of all non-white women rather than respecting differences between, for example, black women and Asian American women. Jacqueline Grant argues that black women are in the process of becoming subjects and learning to resist their being merely regarded as objects defined through their relationship with white men and women as well as black men.[24]

The main way of doing womanist theology is the telling and retelling of the history of oppression and resistance through the stories of women. Womanist theologians are also critical of the sexist bias in the work of black theologians that simply ignores the experiences of women in the black community. An example of this critique is the rejection of the uncritical identification of black theologians with the Hebrew scriptures. This identification understands God as being on the side of the oppressed and marginalized. It remains, however, uncritical of sexism in the Hebrew scriptures as well as the justifications of slavery that can be found in the Hebrew Bible. These are unacceptable in the light of the history of oppression and resistance of black American women.

Mujerista theology describes the theological praxis of Latina or Hispanic women for their own liberation. The name *mujerista* is derived from the Spanish word *mujer,* woman. Ada María Isasi-Díaz describes the goals of *mujerista* theology as follows:

> to provide a platform for the voices of Latina grassroots women; to develop a theological method that takes seriously the religious understandings, church teachings, and religious practices that oppress Latina women, that are not life-giving, and, therefore, cannot be theologically correct.[25]

24. Jaqueline Grant, "Subjectification as a Requirement in Christological Construction," in *Lift Every Voice: Constructing Christian Theologies from the Underside,* ed. Susan Brooks Thistlethwaite and M. P. Engel (San Francisco: Harper & Row, 1990).

25. Ada María Isasi-Díaz, *Mujerista Theology: A Theology for the Twenty-First Century* (Maryknoll, N.Y.: Orbis, 1996), p. 1.

Mujerista theology is not a theology for Latinas, but a theological voice with which Latinas speak for themselves and from their own experiences. Latina women experience themselves as victims of multilayered oppression in the form of sexism, racism, and ethnic prejudice. Doing theology is understood as liberating praxis in the context of Christianity, which has always been an important dimension of Hispanic culture. The text and context of *mujerista* theology are the daily lives of Hispanic women. *Mujerista* theology seeks to advocate Latina women as moral agents and to empower them for their daily struggle for survival and a better future. If the daily lives of women can be considered the location of the liberating praxis that Latina theology advocates, these lives themselves can be considered good, valuable, and salvific. Liberation itself becomes the criterion by which the daily experiences of women in the Hispanic communities are judged. *Mujerista* theology understands itself as a subversion of mainstream theology. It no longer recognizes the normativity of mainstream theologies, but advocates Hispanic women not only as the objects of theology, but as subjects or agents of making theological sense of their own experiences:

> . . . good theology for us *mujerista* theologians is a theology that helps our people in their struggle for survival, not a theology that receives the blessing of the status quo because it follows traditional patterns.[26]

Mujerista anthropology, for instance, is centered around the key elements of the lives of Hispanic women: the struggle *(la lucha),* the right to speak (and to be heard), and the community or (extended) family. It essentially proclaims Hispanic women as human beings in time and history.

Mujerista theology is not so much the work of individual academic theologians, but rather a process that happens in the community of faith and struggle. This rarely happens through the writing of academic books but, for example, through the celebration of *mujerista* liturgies that are

> opportunities for self-affirmation; they are moments that fill us with hope since, during our liturgies, we are able to give free rein to our way of being; they are moments of celebration of our preferred future in which our ethnicity is not an impediment but a funda-

26. Isasi-Díaz, *Mujerista Theology,* p. 79.

mental element of the society in which we live. *Mujerista* liturgies help us to give birth to ourselves as liberated Hispanic women.[27]

These examples of feminist theologies from different contexts and others listed in the annotated bibliography (see particularly some of the compilations of essays by Ursula King and Virginia Fabella) show that feminist theology has become not only diverse but also increasingly conscious of the particular contexts in which women live and that provide the platform for their theological reflection. Feminist theology seeks to identify what creates and shapes women's lives and spiritualities. In doing that it affirms these identities, but also seeks to cross the boundaries created by a patriarchal social-symbolic order that restricts women's lives. One of these boundaries is a worldview that perceives women only in their relationships with men and thereby does not take account of those women whose most significant relationships, both sexual and non-sexual, are with other women.

Lesbian Feminist Theologies

The importance of a variety of diverse voices within feminist theology includes becoming aware not only of different ethnic and cultural contexts but also of different sexual identities. While black women theologians have pointed out that much feminist theology is still written from the hegemonic perspective of white women, lesbian feminists have argued that most feminist critiques of Christian theology and ethics still remains within an essentially heterosexual framework that remains unaware of the lives and experiences of lesbian and bisexual women. Theologians such as Mary Hunt, Carter Heyward, and Elizabeth Stuart identify heterosexual biases within Christian theology and praxis and create new symbols and metaphors that are informed from their experiences as lesbian women.

One of the primary commitments of feminist theology is to writing a theology that advocates justice. One of the most essential forms of justice, though often trivialized, is sexual justice. This is expressed in the writings of some feminist theologians who attempt to make sense of Christianity, its symbols, and its values from their particular perspective as women who

27. Isasi-Díaz, *Mujerista Theology*, pp. 189f.

56

love women. This goes beyond the mere detection of a strong heterosexist bias in the core symbolism of Christianity. The biblical and Christian tradition identifies the church as the bride of Christ, one of the most fundamental relationships within Christianity. This not only defines woman through her relationship with a man, but also identifies heterosexual marriage as the only normative relationship both in spiritual terms and in terms of what is acceptable for members of the Christian church.

A number of feminist scholars, however, claim that they can no longer find this affirmation of women's lives, their bodies, and their sexualities within Christianity and have therefore decided to leave Christianity. The work they have left behind, with its dialogue of discourses and traditions, remains nevertheless an important part of Christian feminist theology.

Post-Christian Feminisms

On a number of occasions throughout this short introduction to Christian feminist theological thinking I have referred to the fundamental ambiguities that Christianity creates for women: Christianity and the Christian churches are at once locations of women's oppression and marginalization and at the same time spaces where women's liberation is possible and where women are able to create meaningful discourses of faith for themselves. Authors such as the North American feminist philosopher Mary Daly and the British feminist theologian Daphne Hampson understand themselves not so much as non-Christian or even anti-Christian but as post-Christian writers whose work is still engaged with the reasons for which they have opted against Christianity. A third group of women have extended their search for a spirituality meaningful for women: women whose rejection of a male patriarchal God has led them to investigate non-Christian and pre-Christian religions in search of a matriarchal Goddess.

Mary Daly, a North American woman trained in theology and philosophy, argues that not only Christianity, but in fact all religion is but an instrument invented by men to oppress and denigrate women. In order to liberate themselves from male oppression, women have to leave behind all organized religion. Daly documented her journey of moving beyond Roman Catholicism before and after the Second Vatican Council in six books. Her first book, *The Church and the Second Sex,* is one of the first feminist analyses of sexism within the Christian tradition. Yet the author, at the time still a Christian, expresses much of the hope for renewal within the church that was characteristic of the time immediately after the Second Vatican Council.

Some feminist thinkers argue that a spirituality meaningful for women cannot be centered around a male God and a religion that ultimately supports male-dominated power structures that suppress women's spirituality. They argue for a new religion that celebrates and legitimates women's power and enables women's liberation. For example, Z. Budapest proposes a Dianic spirituality that "celebrates the female principle of the universe, the birthing power, as the ultimate sacred power and traces its heritage back to the Goddess worship of the ancient world and the witches of the middle Christian period."[28] Yet feminist Goddess spirituality cannot be understood as either a reversal of patriarchal Christianity or as the reconstruction of a historical matriarchal religion. It rather must be understood as a form of spirituality constructed according to the needs of women. In addition, feminist Goddess spirituality celebrates the goodness of the female body and of the female will, of women's history and heritage, and of women's bonding relationships.

A number of post-Christian and post-patriarchal theologians have introduced the concept of *thealogy,* which seeks to reconstruct the idea of female sacrality in theological terms. It was first coined by Naomi Goldenberg who uses it to refer to the "process and content of reflection upon the divine in female terms." "Thealogy differs from Christian feminism in that it endeavours to begin its reflection in a space beyond patriarchal religion."[29] Thealogy refers to the divine as "the Goddess," but essentially keeps the concept open and fluid. It claims to have overcome the dualism inherent in patriarchal religions such as Christianity. Thealogists argue that women embody the divine within themselves through the reality of their daily lives as women and through women's bodily experiences. They seek to overcome the trivialization and profanization of women's lives in patriarchal religions through reversing the values of these religions.

---

28. Christ, *Laughter of Aphrodite,* p. 50.

29. Lisa Isherwood and Elizabeth Stuart, *Introducing Body Theology* (Sheffield: Sheffield Academic Press, 1998), p. 79.

Critical Discussions of Feminist Theologies

Thealogy shows one form of moving beyond the limitations that feminist theologians impose on themselves by staying within the Christian tradition. In the final section of this short guide, I return to Christianity and point out some of the most important criticisms made about the methodologies and approaches used by feminist theologians. Again, it is only possible to present a few exemplary case studies.

Major criticisms have come from conservative Roman Catholic (and Anglican) authors such as Francis Martin and William Oddie. Martin sees feminist theology as rooted in the liberal tradition of the Enlightenment, which asserts the independence of human beings from God. As such it questions not only the order of creation but also sets human understanding above divine inspiration. Martin bases his critique of the *Feminist Question* within the framework of the debate about human rights. In arguing for equal rights for women in the church, women, so Martin, challenge the revealed structures of the church and of doing theology. The challenge posed by feminist theologians, according to Martin, is rooted in the Enlightenment critique of Christianity that has resulted in three fundamental errors of modernity and "must be corrected if feminism is to have a dialogue with revelation. These errors are foundationalism and representationalism in epistemology, and individualism in anthropology."[30] According to Martin, feminism "places experience as the matrix and norm of knowledge." Experience rather than divine revelation becomes the starting point for doing theology. This epistemological foundationalism and representationalism underlie, according to Martin, feminist biblical hermeneutics and feminist approaches to the divine. Martin criticizes feminist reconsiderations of personhood as inherently individualistic while true personhood, he claims, can only be found in relation and essentially in the church, "since it joins heaven and earth and portrays the immortality that gives a person his or her ultimate meaning."[31] Martin's critique, though it appears to be thorough and somewhat groundbreaking, remains, however, limited to the liberal egalitarian feminism of the early years. Martin does not take into account the more recent developments

30. Francis Martin, *The Feminist Question: Feminist Theology in the Light of the Christian Tradition* (Grand Rapids: Eerdmans and Edinburgh: T. & T. Clark, 1994), p. xvi.
31. Martin, *The Feminist Question*, p. xvii.

within feminist theology that are critical of the notion of women's experience and certainly not individualistic but rather based on a concept of interdependence, relationality, and connectedness.

Austrian biblical scholar Susanne Heine attacks feminist theologians for making their own prejudices and negative experiences the basis of their critique of Christianity rather than academic rigor and a well-thought-out methodology. Heine criticizes feminist theology (though she is not very specific about what she means by this term) for seeking a justification from the past for their present ideas. She accuses feminist theologians of "methodicide." Her critique comes from the angle of both early church history and systematic theology. Early Christianity and the Goddess cults that some feminist theologians try to re-employ, so Heine, are far more ambiguous than feminist scholars pretend. Heine calls for scientific exactness in assessing the findings of feminist scholars: "exactness in the historical and systematic-theological sense; exactness in discerning methods and making a critical estimation of what they can and what they cannot do in any particular situation."[32]

Both Francis Martin and Susanne Heine approach their critique of feminist theology from outside the actual debate. They apply scientific and theological paradigms in their critique that are not dissimilar to the ones that feminist theologians have sought to overcome. However, in the late 1990s, much significant critique came from within. Not only has feminist theological scholarship become much more diverse than it initially was, but a new generation has begun to question some of the presuppositions that the first generations of feminist theologians had taken for granted. The Finnish scholar Elina Vuola has provided a thorough critique of the use of liberation theologies by feminist theologians and the applicability of the concept of the "primacy of praxis" with regard to the actual situations in which women live. One of the most thorough discussions of feminist theological methodology has come from Mary McClintock Fulkerson. Fulkerson sees the limitations of feminist theology in the almost exclusive concern with some women's discourses of faith while others, which exist within the framework of the patriarchy that feminist theology resists, are simply overlooked. Fulkerson illustrates this with two case studies of Presbyterian housewives and Black Pentecostal women preachers. Fulkerson provides a

---

32. Susanne Heine, *Women and Early Christianity: Are the Feminist Scholars Right?* (London: SCM, 1986), p. 6.

detailed discussion of feminist biblical hermeneutics that shows feminist scholars have so far worked within the same frameworks as traditional patriarchal scholarship, i.e., an academic context and a methodology that is simply not accessible to a wide variety of women — for whom feminist theology therefore does not appear to speak. Fulkerson argues for feminist theology to open its canon and to take into account a much wider variety of women's discourses of faith. This would then enable a form of feminist scholarship that would truly live up to values such as diversity and attention to particularity that feminist theologians proclaim.

Feminist theology, at the beginning of the new millennium and at the end of the first thirty years of its existence, finds itself in constant process of development and critical dialogue. Feminist theologians are aiming to make a vital contribution to theological reflection within the whole body of Christ rather than providing a marginal discourse or some form of academic luxury. This involves an ongoing critical dialogue with new and traditional forms of theological reflection as well as the kind of self-critique that scholars like Fulkerson provide.

And What about Men . . . ?

In this book I have given a short introduction to the main ideas and concepts used by feminist theologians. It is mainly an invitation to the reader to explore some of the books and articles suggested in the annotated bibliography. One question, however, remains open: What about men? Are feminist scholars simply arguing that after two thousand or more years of male domination, it is not time to focus exclusively on women?

Feminist theology has put some very important questions to the arena of doing Christian theology. These are, however, not merely about women's involvement, inclusion, and points of view, but more generally about the way in which the Christian tradition has constructed and created sexual identities for both women and men. It aims at an understanding of church and society in which men and women can be who they are and be human together. Male theologians such as James Nelson and Richard Rohr have begun to ask questions about maleness and masculinity similar to those asked by feminist theologians, but much more work needs to be done in this area. The beginnings, however, show that ultimately doing theology is an endeavor for the whole Christian community, female and male together.

Annotated Bibliography

This list is limited to works in English that are either of particular importance or particularly helpful to those unfamiliar with the literature.

Introductions and General Readers

Carmody, Denise Lardner. *Christian Feminist Theology: A Constructive Interpretation.* Oxford: Blackwell, 1995.

A useful introductory textbook that seeks to combine some liberal feminist ideas of equality and justice with Christian orthodoxy. The author develops a new concept of theology based on viewing the Christian tradition and liberal egalitarian feminist ideas as reconcilable.

Chopp, Rebecca. "Feminist and Womanist Theologies," in *The Modern Theologians: An Introduction to Christian Theology in the Twentieth Century,* edited by David Ford. Oxford: Blackwell, 1997, pp. 389-404.

A useful introductory article covering the most important aspects of feminist theological methodology. It is accompanied by a short bibliography of primary and secondary sources.

Fiorenza, Elisabeth Schüssler, ed. *The Power of Naming: A Concilium Reader in Feminist Liberation Theology.* London: SCM, 1996.

A wide-ranging reader that originated from two volumes of the journal *Concilium,* introducing the work of feminist theologians from different contexts and documenting the history and development of feminist theology over thirty years.

Isherwood, Lisa, and Dorothea McEwan. *Introducing Feminist Theology.* Sheffield: Sheffield Academic Press, 1993, new edition 2001.

A very basic introduction of the most important ideas and methods, written for a non-academic audience. Excellent first book to put in the hands of people new to the issues.

Isherwood, Lisa, and Dorothea McEwan. *An A-Z of Feminist Theology.* Sheffield: Sheffield Academic Press, 1996.

A useful handbook/dictionary with articles on a wide variety of topics relevant to feminist theology.

Kalven, Janet, and Mary I. Buckley. *Women's Spirit Bonding.* New York: Pilgrim, 1984.

A reader that surveys a variety of different types of women's discourses of faith within and outside Christianity. Interesting, though somewhat dated. The collection focuses on feminist theology and ethics in a wider social context, discussing issues such as poverty, peace, and the environment.

LaCugna, Catherine Mowry, ed. *Freeing Theology: The Essentials of Theology in Feminist Perspective.* San Francisco: Harper & Row, 1993.

A reader that covers the key *loci* of systematic theology from a feminist perspective. It contains a number of useful introductory articles on particular topics such as Christology and the sacraments as well as useful bibliographies. All contributors are from a Roman Catholic background and combine a critique of the Christian tradition with the attempt to unearth the liberating elements within the tradition. Contributors include Sandra Schneiders, Elizabeth Johnson, and Joann Wolski Conn.

Loades, Ann. *Searching for Lost Coins: Explorations on Christianity and Feminism.* London: SPCK, 1987.

Another basic introduction that combines feminist theological ideas and the search for women in the Christian tradition.

Loades, Ann, ed. *Feminist Theology: A Reader.* London: SPCK, 1990.

A classic reader that covers a wide range of the early ideas of feminist theologians, but is restricted to white European and North American feminist theology. With an extensive introduction and commentaries on individual chapters, this reader provides a very useful overview of feminist theological writing in dialogue with the Christian tradition during the 1980s. Contributors include Rosemary Radford Ruether, Phyllis Trible, Elisabeth Schüssler Fiorenza, and Sallie McFague.

Plaskow, Judith. *Standing Again at Sinai: Judaism from a Feminist Perspective.* San Francisco: Harper & Row, 1990.

A classic text for feminist theology from a Jewish perspective that challenges sexism and androcentrism within the Jewish tradition, but argues for the possibility of writing women into the covenant and the Jewish tradition that cannot exist without them. Plaskow proposes a new theology of women's sexuality within a Jewish framework of covenant and tradition.

Plaskow, Judith, and Carol Christ, eds. *Womanspirit Rising.* San Francisco: Harper & Row, 1992.

A classic reader that covers both a variety of Christian and non-Christian approaches to theology and spirituality in a liberal feminist paradigm. Sections include: "The Past: Does It Hold a Future for Women?," "Does Theology Speak to Women's Experience?," "Reconstructing Tradition," and "Creating New Traditions."

Ruether, Rosemary Radford. *Sexism and God-Talk: Toward a Feminist Theology.* Boston: Beacon, 1983.

An early and influential overview of a critical re-reading and re-writing of the Christian tradition from a liberal feminist perspective that covers a variety of topics such as Christology, the concept of "usable" texts, and anthropology. A comprehensive introduction to the writing of Rosemary Radford Ruether.

Russell, Letty, and J. Shannon Clarkson, eds. *Dictionary of Feminist Theologies.* Louisville: Westminster/John Knox, 1996.

A dictionary that summarizes the developments of feminist theological thinking, mainly though not exclusively from a range of North American perspectives. Useful and readable articles combined with a comprehensive bibliography make this a vital tool for anyone studying feminist theology.

Schneiders, Sandra M. *Beyond Patching: Faith and Feminism in the Catholic Church.* New York: Paulist, 1991.

An introductory text that challenges both praxis and theology of the Roman Catholic Church from the perspective of women's experience. Described as a "very engaging text," the book provides useful overviews of some of the key issues from a Roman Catholic feminist perspective.

Soskice, Janet Martin, ed. *After Eve: Women, Theology and the Christian Tradition*. London: Marshall Pickering, 1990.

A reader that compiles a number of different essays on a variety of topics relevant to the Christian tradition.

Thistlethwaite, Susan Brooks. *Sex, Race and God: Christian Feminism in Black and White*. London: Chapman, 1990.

The author attempts to write white feminist theology against the background of her knowledge of African American history. She asks about the significance of race for doing theology in North America today.

Tulip, Marie, and Erin White, eds. *Knowing Otherwise: Feminism, Women and Religion*. Melbourne: Lovell, 1990.

A wide-ranging introduction into feminist theology and feminist Christian praxis from an Australian perspective.

Young, Pamela Dickey. *Feminist Theology/Christian Theology: In Search of Method*. Minneapolis: Fortress, 1990.

A useful introduction into feminist methodology that discusses the work of authors such as Elisabeth Schüssler Fiorenza and Rosemary Radford Ruether in order to identify a theological paradigm with which feminist theologians can reflect on the Christian tradition.

Weidman, Judith L., ed. *Christian Feminism: Visions of a New Humanity*. San Francisco: Harper & Row, 1984.

A now somewhat dated collection that gives interesting insight into some early feminist discussion of Christian theology.

Feminist Ways of Reading Scripture

Achtemeier, Paul J., ed. "The Bible, Theology and Feminist Approaches," special issue of *Interpretation: A Journal of Bible and Theology* 42, no. 1 (1988).

An overview of different approaches to feminist theological hermeneutics. A helpful introductory survey.

Bach, Alice, ed. *The Pleasure of Her Text: Feminist Readings of Biblical and Historical Texts.* Philadelphia: Trinity Press International, 1990.

A collection of essays on different biblical and historical texts from a variety of feminist perspectives. A good anthology of readings.

Bal, Mieke. *Lethal Love: Feminist Literary Readings of Biblical Love Stories.* Bloomington: Indiana University Press, 1987.

A monograph focusing on biblical love stories using feminist biblical hermeneutics informed by literary theory.

Bal, Mieke, ed. *Anti-Covenant: Counter-Reading Women's Lives.* Sheffield: Sheffield Academic Press, 1989.

A collection of essays on different women in the Bible and the way the Bible has influenced the lives of women throughout the Christian and Jewish traditions.

Bellis, A. O. *Helpmates, Harlots, Heroes: Women's Stories in the Hebrew Bible.* Louisville: Westminster/John Knox, 1994.

A feminist theological reading of the lives of women in the Hebrew scriptures. Suitable as an introduction to feminist readings of the Hebrew Bible.

Bird, Phyllis. *The Bible as the Church's Book.* Philadelphia: Westminster, 1982.

A feminist discussion of the use of the Bible and its impact on women's lives in the history and the present praxis of the Christian churches.

Brenner, Athalya, and Fokkelien van Dijk-Hermes. *On Gendering Texts: Female and Male Voices in the Hebrew Bible.* Biblical Interpretation Series 1. Leiden: Brill, 1993.

A collection of essays on different characters from a variety of books in the Hebrew Bible from a perspective informed by feminist theology and theological gender studies.

Brenner, Athalya, and Carole Fontaine. *A Feminist Companion to Reading the Bible: Approaches, Methods and Strategies.* Sheffield: Sheffield Academic Press, 1997.

The most comprehensive and wide-ranging introduction to different approaches of feminist biblical hermeneutics, the feminist study of particular texts, and particular topics such as anti-Semitism.

Cannon, Katie, and Elisabeth Schüssler Fiorenza. *Interpretation for Liberation.* Atlanta: Scholars Press, 1989.

An introduction to feminist biblical hermeneutics informed by liberation theology and liberal feminisms from both black and white perspectives.

Collins, Adela Yarbro. *Feminist Perspectives on Biblical Scholarship.* Society of Biblical Literature Centennial Publications. Atlanta: Scholars Press, 1985.

An overview of different feminist approaches to reading Scripture.

Exum, J. Cheryl. *Fragmented Women: Feminist Subversions of Biblical Narratives.* JSOT Supplement Series 163. Sheffield: Sheffield Academic Press, 1993.

A reading informed by feminist literary criticism of the stories of different women, named and unnamed, in the Hebrew Bible. Presumes knowledge of feminist literary theory, but nevertheless very readable as an introduction to this particular form of feminist critical reading of Scripture.

Exum, J. Cheryl. *Plotted, Shot and Painted: Cultural Representations of Biblical Women.* JSOT Supplement Series 215. Sheffield: Sheffield Academic Press, 1996.

A feminist critical evaluation of representations of biblical women in media such as literature and film. An interesting example of the use of feminist literary critical hermeneutics.

Fiorenza, Elisabeth Schüssler. *Bread Not Stone: The Challenge of Feminist Biblical Interpretation.* Boston: Beacon, 1984.

A useful introduction to Fiorenza's approach to feminist liberationist interpretation of Scripture and its impact on women's lives and experiences.

Fiorenza, Elisabeth Schüssler. *But She Said: Feminist Practices of Biblical Interpretation.* Boston: Beacon, 1992.

An introduction and overview of Fiorenza's approach to reading and proclaiming the Bible and women's lives in it as part of a feminist liberation theology.

Fiorenza, Elisabeth Schüssler. *Sharing Her Word: Feminist Biblical Interpretation in Context.* Edinburgh: T. & T. Clark and Boston: Beacon, 1998.

An extension and further development of the author's approach to feminist liberation hermeneutics and its application to a variety of different topics. Fiorenza suggests a sevenfold feminist hermeneutical paradigm: "a hermeneutics of experience that socially locates experience, a hermeneutics of domination, a hermeneutics of suspicion, a hermeneutics of assessment and evaluation, a hermeneutics of reimagination, a hermeneutics of reconstruction, and a hermeneutics of change and transformation."

Fiorenza, Elisabeth Schüssler, ed. *Searching the Scriptures I: A Feminist Introduction.* New York: Crossroads, 1993.

A wide-ranging collection of essays introducing different approaches to feminist interpretation of the Christian scriptures. Published to mark the centenary of the *Women's Bible* and aiming to overcome its limitations in terms of representing Black, Asian, and Latina women as well as women from a European context and using different methodologies.

Laffey, Alice L. *Wives, Harlots and Concubines: The Old Testament in Feminist Perspective.* London: SPCK, 1988.

An introduction to the feminist interpretation of the Hebrew scriptures. Suitable as an introduction to the topic.

Moltmann-Wendel, Elisabeth. *The Women around Jesus.* New York: Crossroads, 1982.

One of the early feminist approaches to the gospels and the female characters in them.

Ostriker, A. *Feminist Revision of the Bible.* Oxford: Blackwell, 1993.

An introductory textbook on feminist hermeneutics of Scripture.

Parales, Heidi Bright. *Hidden Voices: Biblical Women and Our Christian Heritage.* Macon, Ga.: Smyth & Helwys, 1998.

A discussion of issues such as anti-Judaism and sexism in the Christian tradition of reading Scripture.

Pobee, J. S., and B. von Wartenberg-Potter, eds. *New Eyes for Reading: Biblical and Theological Reflections by Women from the Third World.* Geneva: WCC, 1986.

A collection of basic introductions to feminist reading of the Bible from the perspectives of women in the Third World.

Russell, Letty, ed. *Feminist Interpretation of the Bible.* Philadelphia: Westminster, 1995.

A collection of essays introducing different approaches to the feminist interpretation of the Bible. A good introduction, though somewhat dated now.

Schneiders, Sandra. *The Revelatory Text: Interpreting the New Testament as Sacred Scripture.* San Francisco: Harper & Row, 1991.

An scholarly introduction to Sandra Schneiders's approach to a feminist Christian interpretation of the New Testament.

Schottroff, Luise. *Let the Oppressed Go Free: Feminist Perspectives on the New Testament.* Louisville: Westminster/John Knox, 1995.

This discussion of feminist perspectives on the Christian scriptures is informed by liberation theology and German political theology. It is a scholarly introduction to feminist hermeneutics and its significance for working towards justice and peace.

Tamez, Elsa. *Bible of the Oppressed.* Maryknoll, N.Y.: Orbis, 1982.

Introduction to reading Scripture from the perspective of Latin American women.

Tolbert, Mary Ann. *The Bible and Feminist Hermeneutics.* Chico, Calif.: Scholars Press, 1983.

Useful, though somewhat limited and dated, introduction to feminist biblical hermeneutics.

Trible, Phyllis. *God and the Rhetoric of Sexuality.* Philadelphia: Fortress, 1978.

This book is still considered one of the key texts regarding a feminist reading of the Hebrew Bible. Using feminist literary criticism as her methodological basis, Trible searches for "neglected themes and counter literature."

Trible, Phyllis. *Texts of Terror: Literary-Feminist Readings of Biblical Narratives.* Philadelphia: Fortress, 1984.

An introduction to reading some of the difficult texts of the Hebrew Bible dealing with women and how they have shaped the image of women and women's experiences in the Christian tradition. Another key text.

Weems, Renita. *Just a Sister Away: A Womanist Vision of Women's Relationships in the Bible.* San Diego: Lura Media, 1988.

A black feminist reading of Scripture.

Feminist Bible Commentaries

Brenner, Athalya, ed. *A Feminist Companion to Genesis.* The Feminist Companion to the Bible 2. Sheffield: Sheffield Academic Press, 1993.

Brenner, Athalya, ed. *A Feminist Companion to Ruth.* The Feminist Companion to the Bible 3. Sheffield: Sheffield Academic Press, 1993.

Brenner, Athalya, ed. *A Feminist Companion to Exodus to Deuteronomy.* The Feminist Companion to the Bible 6. Sheffield: Sheffield Academic Press, 1994.

Brenner, Athalya, ed. *A Feminist Companion to Esther, Judith and Susanna.* The Feminist Companion to the Bible 7. Sheffield: Sheffield Academic Press, 1995.

Brenner, Athalya, ed. *A Feminist Companion to the Latter Prophets.* The Feminist Companion to the Bible 8. Sheffield: Sheffield Academic Press, 1995.

Brenner, Athalya, ed. *A Feminist Companion to Wisdom Literature.* The Feminist Companion to the Bible 9. Sheffield: Sheffield Academic Press, 1995.

Brenner, Athalya, ed. *A Feminist Companion to the Hebrew Bible in the New Testament.* The Feminist Companion to the Bible 10. Sheffield: Sheffield Academic Press, 1996.

The *Feminist Companion* series contains a number of useful collections of essays on particular books of the Hebrew scriptures. Very helpful in working on a particular text.

Camp, Claudia. *Wisdom and the Feminine in the Book of Proverbs.* JSOT Supplement Series. Sheffield: Sheffield Academic Press, 1985.

The key text on feminist exegetical study of the concept of wisdom in the Hebrew Bible.

Fiorenza, Elisabeth Schüssler, ed. *Searching the Scriptures II: A Feminist Commentary.* New York: Crossroads, 1994.

The second volume of *Searching the Scriptures* contains a wide variety of introductory essays on different types of feminist readings of both canonical and non-canonical texts of the first centuries. A valuable tool in doing feminist exegesis. Contains useful bibliographies on individual texts.

Kates, J. A., and G. T. Reimer, eds. *Reading Ruth: Contemporary Women Reclaim a Sacred Story.* New York: Ballantine, 1994.

A feminist discussion of the book of Ruth.

Newsom, Carol A., and Sharon H. Ringe, eds. *The Women's Bible Commentary.* Louisville: Westminster/John Knox, 1992.

A collection of introductory essays on different canonical books of the Hebrew and the Christian scriptures. Very useful tool.

Wainwright, Elaine M. *Toward a Feminist Critical Reading of the Gospel according to Matthew.* Berlin: de Gruyter, 1991.

A feminist commentary on the Gospel of Matthew.

Weems, Renita. *Battered Love: Marriage, Sex and Violence in the Hebrew Prophets.* Minneapolis: Fortress, 1995.

A feminist introduction to the Hebrew prophets and the portrayal of women in their writings.

Wire, A. C. *The Corinthian Women Prophets: A Reconstruction through Paul's Rhetoric.* Minneapolis: Fortress, 1990.

A feminist reading of Paul's letter to the Corinthians using feminist rhetorical criticism.

Women's History and the Development of Feminist Theology

Bynum, Caroline Walker. *Jesus as Mother: Studies in the Spirituality of the High Middle Ages.* Berkeley: University of California Press, 1982.

The author describes the importance of late medieval women mystics as primarily responsible for "encouraging and propagating some of the most distinctive aspects of late medieval piety: devotion to the human, especially the infant, Christ, and devotion to the Eucharist frequently focused in devotion to the wounds, blood, body and heart of Jesus" (p. 172).

Bynum, Caroline Walker. *Holy Feast and Holy Fast: The Religious Significance of Food to Medieval Women.* Berkeley: University of California Press, 1987.

Bynum's work is one of the most important contributions to the study of medieval women's lives. Influential and learned.

Byrne, Lavinia. *Women Before God.* London: SPCK, 1988.

A collection of texts written by women from different ages of the history of the church.

Clark, Elizabeth A. *Women in the Early Church.* Wilmington, Del.: Michael Glazier, 1983.

A collection of primary sources regarding the role and ministries of women in the earliest centuries of the Christian church.

Cloke, Gillian. *"This Female Man of God": Women and Spiritual Power in the Patristic Age.* London and New York: Routledge, 1995.

An important contribution to the study of the age of the church fathers, their attitudes to women, and women's responses to them.

Daly, Mary. *The Church and the Second Sex.* New York: Harper & Row, 1975.

One of the earliest contributions to feminist theology. Daly, still at that time within Roman Catholic Christianity, evaluates the relationship between men and women in the Roman Catholic Church and makes suggestions for transformation.

Fiorenza, Elisabeth Schüssler. *In Memory of Her: A Feminist Theological Reconstruction of Christian Origins,* 2nd ed. London: SCM, 1993.

A classic critical study of the role of women in the earliest Christian churches and the sources about them, which forms the basis of a new feminist ecclesiology. Fiorenza challenges previous conceptions of early Christianity as being distorted by patriarchal scholarship. Fiorenza describes the earliest Christian communities as followers of the vision of Jesus, which was one of equality and justice. Fiorenza argues that, even though this vision has been distorted by patriarchal scholarship, it has never entirely vanished and can therefore be re-visioned for the restoration of the church today. It is, however, important to bear in mind that Fiorenza does not understand her conception of early Christianity as a movement in which equality and social justice prevailed as an *archetype* that can be *re-enacted,* but rather as *prototype* of a vision that needs to be *re-visioned* in order to be embodied in the church of the future.

Irigaray, Luce. "Equal to Whom?," *Differences* 1, no. 2 (1988): 59-76.

An interesting critical discussion of Fiorenza's *In Memory of Her* from the perspective of a French feminist philosopher.

Jantzen, Grace M. *Julian of Norwich: Mystic and Theologian.* London: SPCK and New York: Paulist, 1987.

A biography and introduction to the writings of one of the most important medieval women writers.

McEnroy, Carmel. *Guests in Their Own House: The Women of Vatican II.* New York: Crossroad, 1996.

An interesting account of the neglect of women as well as of the women present at the Second Vatican Council.

McHaffie, Barbara. *Her Story: Women in the Christian Tradition.* Philadelphia: Fortress, 1986.

A key introduction to feminist church history.

McLaughlin, Eleanor, and Rosemary Radford Ruether, eds. *Women of Spirit: Female Leadership in the Jewish and Christian Traditions.* New York: Simon and Schuster, 1979.

A collection of essays about women in ministry and leadership in different Jewish and Christian traditions.

Ranke-Heinemann, Uta. *Eunuchs for the Kingdom of Heaven.* Garden City: Doubleday, 1990.

An evaluation of attitudes to sexuality in the Roman Catholic Church.

Ruether, Rosemary Radford. *Women and Redemption: A Theological History.* London: SCM, 1998.

A history of theology from an ecofeminist perspective, based on the study of both primary and secondary sources.

Schottroff, Luise. *Lydia's Impatient Sisters: A Feminist Social History of Early Christianity.* Translated by Barbara and Martin Rumscheidt. Louisville: Westminster/John Knox, 1995.

An introduction to the study of women's participation and attitudes to women in the earliest Christian centuries and their relevance for women in the Christian churches today.

Tucker, Ruth. *Daughters of the Church: A History of Women in Ministry.* Grand Rapids: Zondervan, 1987.

An extensive history of women's ministry in different Christian churches.

Weaver, Mary Jo. *New Catholic Women: A Contemporary Challenge to Traditional Religious Authority.* San Francisco: Harper & Row, 1985.

A history of women challenging sexism and exclusion from the Roman Catholic Church in the second half of the twentieth century and creating their own discourses of faith within it.

Witherington III, Ben. *Women in the Earliest Churches.* SNTS Monograph Series 59. New York: Cambridge University Press, 1988.

An introduction to the participation of women in the life of the earliest Christian communities.

Witherington III, Ben. *Women and the Genesis of Christianity.* Cambridge: Cambridge University Press, 1990.

An introduction to the significance of women in the development of early Christian doctrine and praxis. This volume is a summary of his more scholarly work in earlier monographs.

Wood, Diana, and W. J. Sheils. *Women in the Church.* Oxford: Blackwell, 1990.

A collection of essays on women in different periods of Christian history.

In Search of Criteria: Feminist Theological Approaches to the Christian Tradition

Carmody, Denise Lardner. *Christian Feminist Theology: A Constructive Interpretation.* Oxford: Blackwell, 1995.

A useful introductory textbook that seeks to combine some liberal feminist ideas of equality and justice with Christian orthodoxy. Seeks to reclaim the Christian tradition from a feminist perspective.

Carr, Ann E. *Tranforming Grace: Christian Tradition and Women's Experience.* San Francisco: Harper & Row, 1988.

One of the earlier overviews of Roman Catholic feminist theology that covers a range of topic such as the situation of women in the Roman Catholic Church, Christology, and theological anthropology.

Grey, Mary. *The Wisdom of Fools: Seeking Revelation for Today.* London: SPCK, 1993.

Suitable as an introduction. Grey asks about the reality of women having been excluded from the concept of revelation, both with regard to defining what counts as revealed truth and from the main teaching bodies of the church. Grey proposes "connectedness," a motif found in the work of a number of feminist theologians, as a new metaphor for Christian revelation. This means that "revelation" must be understood as the process of becoming aware of one's being in relation not only to other human beings, but also to the whole of creation. Being connected, being in relation, involves the challenge to work towards right relationship, to live in harmony with creation as the space where God reveals Godself.

von Kellenbach, Katharina. *Anti-Judaism in Feminist Religious Writings.* The American Academy of Religion, 1994.

Jewish feminist von Kellenbach identifies an anti-Semitic bias of some Christian feminist theologies. Jesus and the early Christian movement are at times portrayed as standing in radical contrast to the Jewish background from which they developed. This can be problematic, not least in the light of the connection between Christian anti-Semitism and the Holocaust. Judaism is reduced to being an antithesis to the liberating reality of the early Christian movement; Judaism is at times accused of inventing the archetypal patriarchal religion or it is simply understood as being superseded by Jesus, the liberator of women. In taking up one or more of these possible interpretations, feminist theologians reiterate one of the most destructive elements of patriarchal theologies. Von Kellenbach challenges Christian feminists to take the distinctive nature of Judaism seriously while acknowledging the common heritage of Judaism and Christianity. She argues that feminism must not be used to deny the differences between Judaism and Christianity, but to work with them in a constructive way that is equally affirming to Jewish-identified feminists and to feminists from the Christian tradition.

Mollenkott, Virginia Ramey. *The Divine Feminine: The Biblical Imagery of God as Female.* New York: Crossroad, 1983.

A now somewhat dated introduction to a theology that is informed by both feminism and Evangelical Christianity.

Ruether, Rosemary Radford. *Faith and Fratricide: The Theological Roots of Anti-Semitism.* Boston: Seabury, 1974.

A discussion of anti-Semitism within the Christian tradition from a liberal feminist theological perspective.

Ruether, Rosemary Radford. *Women and Redemption: A Theological History.* London: SCM, 1998.

A history of Christian theology and the factors that have influenced it throughout its history from a feminist perspective. Good overview and introduction.

Critical Discourses of Transformation: Feminist Re-Readings of Theology

1. Theology, Androcentrism, Sex, and Gender

Atkinson, Clarissa W., Constance H. Buchanan, and Margaret R. Miles, eds. *Immaculate and Powerful: The Female in Sacred Image and Social Reality.* Harvard Women's Studies in Religion Series. New York: Harper & Row, 1985.

A collection of interesting essays on a variety of topics from within and outside Christianity, written by theologians and scholars from other disciplines.

Atkinson, Clarissa W., Constance H. Buchanan, and Margaret R. Miles, eds. *Shaping New Vision: Gender and Values in American Culture.* Harvard Women's Studies in Religion Series. Ann Arbor: UMI Research Press, 1987.

In many ways a sequel to the previous item, though more narrowly focused on American culture.

Becher, Jeanne, ed. *Women, Religion and Sexuality: Studies on the Impact of Religious Teachings on Women.* Geneva: WCC, 1990.

This collection is the result of a colloquium organized by the Women's Desk of the World Council of Churches. It is aimed at a non-academic audience and provides a wide variety of different contributions reflecting women's experiences from different cultures all over the world.

Borrowdale, Anne. *Distorted Images: Christian Attitudes to Women, Men and Sex.* London: SPCK, 1991.

A discussion of gender stereotypes within contemporary Western culture, the Christian tradition, and the life of the church, highlighting sexual violence against women in particular. Good introductory reading regarding issues of gender constructions and their impact on women's lives.

Brenner, Athalya, and Fokkelien van Dijk-Hemmes, eds. *Reflections on Theology and Gender.* Kampen: Kok/Pharos, 1995.

A collection of essays from authors representing a variety of theological disciplines as well as women's studies.

Carr, Anne, and Elisabeth Schüssler Fiorenza, eds. *The Special Nature of Women?* Edinburgh: T. & T. Clark, 1991.

Originally a volume of the journal *Concilium,* this collection provides a number of easy-to-read introductory essays regarding gender constructions within the Christian tradition and their impact on women's lives within the Christian churches.

Erikson, Anne-Louise. *The Meaning of Gender in Theology.* Uppsala: Almqvist and Wiksell International, 1995.

Though difficult to obtain outside Sweden, this is probably the most important and the most theological discussion of the concept of gender and its significance for theological reflection. A vital contribution to the theological discussion of gender.

Graham, Elaine. *Making the Difference: Gender, Personhood and Theology.* London: Mowbray, 1995.

An important volume that makes different approaches to the concept of gender accessible to theologians, though the discussion of the significance of gender for theology remains rather limited. A useful introduction.

Graham, Elaine. "Making the Difference: Gender, Personhood and Theology," *Scottish Journal of Theology* 48, no. 3 (1995): 341-58.

A summary of the arguments of the previous item.

Hurcombe, Linda, ed. *Sex and God: Some Varieties of Women's Religious Experience.* London: Routledge, Chapman and Hall, 1987.

A collection of essays discussing the impact of gender constructions, sexual stereotypes, and androcentrism in the Christian tradition and in the life of the church today.

Keller, Catherine. *From a Broken Web: Separation, Sexism and Self.* Boston: Beacon, 1986.

A discussion of the impact of gender constructions and sexual stereotyping in both Christian theology and mythology. More suitable for readers who already have a certain amount of knowledge about feminist thinking and Christian theology.

Kim, C. W. Maggie, et al. *Transfigurations: Theology and the French Feminists.* Minneapolis: Fortress, 1993.

An important, though not easy to read, collection of essays on the impact and the significance of French feminist thinkers such as Irigaray and Kristeva and their concept of sexual difference for feminist theology. Presumes knowledge of both French feminist theory and the work of a number of feminist theologians.

King, Ursula, ed. *Religion and Gender.* Oxford: Blackwell, 1995.

This useful and comprehensive collection of essays discussing the concept of gender and its significance for religious studies is nevertheless interesting and useful for theologians. The essays cover a wide range of subjects and give valuable insights not only into the study of gender, but also into feminist and gender studies approaches to religions other than Christianity.

Lloyd, Genevieve. *This Man of Reason: 'Male' and 'Female' in Western Philosophy.* London: Routledge, 1984.

One of the early though nevertheless still important surveys of the impact of dualistic gender constructions on the philosophical schools of thought that have informed and still inform our theological thinking. A good introductory overview.

O'Grady, Jane, Janette Gray, and Ann Gilroy, eds. *Bodies, Lives, Voices: Gender in Theology.* Sheffield: Sheffield Academic Press, 1997.

A wide-ranging collection of essays that discuss the impact of gender constructions on different aspects of Christian theology and theological methodology.

Ruether, Rosemary Radford. *New Woman, New Earth: Sexist Ideologies and Human Liberation.* Boston: Seabury, 1975.

One of the early monographs on ecofeminism and the impact of dualistic gender constructions on all aspects of Western culture and the image of women within it. Somewhat dated, but still important for the study of the development of the theology of Rosemary Radford Ruether and American feminist theology in general.

Schmidt, A. *Veiled and Silenced: How Cultures Shaped Sexist Theology.* Macon, Ga.: Mercer University Press, 1989.

A useful introductory monograph on the relationship between theology, culture, and sexism.

Van Leeuwen, M. S., ed. *After Eden: Facing the Challenge of Gender Reconciliation.* Grand Rapids: Eerdmans, 1993.

An interdisciplinary study of the impact of gender relations and their distortion on all aspects of life. A wide-ranging introduction from a perspective informed by both feminism and Reformed Christianity.

Webster, Alison. *Found Wanting: Women, Christianity and Sexuality.* London: Cassell, 1995.

An interesting study based on a wide range of interviews with women primarily from Reformed and Protestant traditions discussing the impact of distorted views of sexuality and sexual experiences on the lives of women in Christian churches. Aimed at both academic and non-academic readers.

2. Beyond the Maleness of God: Rethinking Male God-Language

Anderson, Sherry R., and Patricia Hopkins. *The Feminine Face of God.* New York: Bantam, 1991.

An evaluation of feminine imagery of the divine used in Scripture and the Christian tradition.

Bondi, Roberta C. "'Be Not Afraid': Praying to God the Father," *Modern Theology* 9, no. 3 (1993): 235-48.

An exploration of the theme of divine fatherhood and its implication for prayer and spirituality in the light of different experiences with human fathers.

Børreson, K. E. *The Image of God: Gender Models in the Judaeo-Christian Tradition.* Minneapolis: Fortress, 1995.

An evaluation of the impact of gendered images of both the divine and the human in the Jewish and the Christian tradition and their impact on women based on thorough research of a wide range of texts.

Case-Winters, A. *God's Power.* Louisville: Westminster/John Knox, 1990.

A feminist discussion of the theme of divine power in the works of John Calvin and other theologians. Presumes a certain amount of knowledge of Calvinist and feminist theology.

Duck, Ruth C. *Gender and the Name of God: The Trinitarian Baptismal Formula.* New York: Pilgrim, 1991.

A useful evaluation of the use of gendered and masculine imagery in the liturgy and its implications for pastoral ministry.

Heyward, Carter. *The Redemption of God: A Theology of Mutual Relation.* Lanham, Md.: University Press of America, 1982.

A discussion of images and concepts of the divine from a lesbian feminist perspective. An important text.

Johnson, Elizabeth A. *She Who Is: The Mystery of God in Feminist Theological Discourse.* New York: Crossroad, 1994.

Probably the most important feminist reappropriation of the symbol of the Trinity. Johnson uses concepts of being and of ontology in order to reconsider the Trinity and the names of the divine in the context of the challenges of feminist theology. While some aspects of the Christian tradition have argued that the Holy Spirit could be understood as the feminine person of the Trinity, Johnson points out that such a concept would reduce the Trinity to being two male persons and one rather elusive female on whom it is easy to project those stereotypes of the feminine that feminist theologians try to oppose. She proposes to understand all three persons of the Trinity through the theme of the divine *sophia* — the Spirit-Sophia, Jesus Sophia, and Mother Sophia. For Johnson, describing each of the persons of the Trinity through the metaphor of divine wisdom helps avoid the use of feminine or masculine stereotypes for individual trinitarian persons and helps reaffirm the feminine in the Trinity. Johnson understands her concept of God as feminine as a deliberate corrective to the dominance of male imagery for the divine.

LaCugna, Catherine Mowry. *God For Us: The Trinity and Christian Life.* San Francisco: Harper & Row, 1991.

This book attempts to reclaim orthodox Christian concepts of God and the Trinity used by the church fathers using some feminist ideas. A scholarly but nevertheless very readable and detailed study.

McFague, Sallie. *Metaphorical Theology: Models of God in Religious Language.* London: SCM, 1982.

A new proposal for God-language and imagery exploring the concept of metaphor in order to develop a theology suitable for the current ecological and nuclear crisis. McFague, one of the most important authors to have written on a feminist renaming of the divine, criticizes the hierarchical model of God as Father of All. She suggests a reconsideration of the Trinity as mother, lover, and friend, and the world as the body of God. This, however, does not mean to replace patriarchal hierarchy with matriarchy, but to discover new dimensions of the relationship between God and world/humanity such as care and nurture. Her reconsiderations of God language are written against the background of the ecological crisis and the fear of a nuclear holocaust at the end of the twentieth century. A concept of God as mother of the earth suggests the interconnectedness and mutuality of all life or an understanding of creation as based on gestation, giving birth, and lactation — expressions of interdependence of creation on the divine. God as mother wants the flourishing of all creation. For McFague, maternal God language can only be one possible way of speaking of God, as it would otherwise run the risk of romanticizing motherhood and mother-child relationships and of reducing women to motherhood, when there are many women who are not mothers. A concept of God as mother needs to be complemented with concepts of God as sister and as lover. McFague also expresses the interdependence of God and world through understanding the world as the body of God. Such a concept of interdependence overcomes the hierarchical dualisms between God and world, the divine and the human, the mind and the body, which are characteristic of patriarchal theology. It also speaks out against the way the female body and the process of childbirth in particular is rendered defiling, impure, and unworthy of the sacred in traditional, patriarchal Christianity. McFague understands theology as fiction, in other words: the elaboration on a number of key metaphors and models. A concept of God that perceives the world as the body of God suggests a paradigm of reality that enables ways of understanding the relationship between God and the world as open, caring, inclusive, interdependent, changing, mutual, and creative. McFague calls for a thorough revision of the metaphors used in Christian God-language. She argues that even metaphors that could suggest a concept of mutuality and independence such as the description of God as father have been so abused through their connection with ideas such as kingship and lordship that their liberating potential is undercut. She proposes a metaphorical theology that distinguishes between metaphorical speech about God and divine reality in order to gain and retain credibility in a nuclear age. Metaphors for God are therefore not descriptions of God, but accounts of experiences with the divine, referring to those relationships known to those who write metaphorical theology. McFague argues that God language is inevitably sexual as human beings who use themselves and their relationships as the basis for their concepts of the divine are sexual beings. To speak of the divine as mother would enable a revaluation of female sexuality as no longer dangerous and defiling, but rather as a source for models of the divine as well as good in human terms. The divine can never be met in an unmediated way, but must always be mediated through human relationships and human language. McFague tries to overcome the distinction between divine transcendence and human immanence. The divine envisaged as mother, lover, and friend is both transcendent and immanent, embodied in the world as God's body.

McFague, Sallie. *Models of God: Theology for an Ecological Nuclear Age.* Philadelphia: Fortress, 1992.

A further development of McFague's theology in the light of the current crisis using feminist and liberation theology as the basis of her explorations.

McFague, Sallie. *The Body of God: An Ecological Theology.* Minneapolis: Fortress, 1993.

In this book, one of the key texts of ecofeminist theology, McFague develops the idea of the world as God's body from an ecofeminist perspective.

Metz, Johannes, and Edward Schillebeeckx, eds. *God as Father?* Concilium 143. Edinburgh: T. & T. Clark, 1981.

This volume of *Concilium* contains a variety of different essays discussing the idea of divine fatherhood and alternatives to it in the light of feminist critique. The essays are short and easy to read.

Mollenkott, Virginia Ramey. *The Divine Feminine: The Biblical Imagery of God as Female.* New York: Crossroad, 1983.

One of Mollenkott's early books that seeks to make feminist theology and its critique of masculine God-language and imagery accessible to an evangelical audience.

Ramshaw, Gail, and J. Walton. *God Beyond Gender: Feminist Christian God-Language.* Minneapolis: Fortress, 1995.

A critique of exclusively masculine God-language by two feminist liturgical scholars.

Soskice, Janet Martin. "Can a Feminist Call God Father?," in *Women's Voices: Essays in Contemporary Feminist Theology,* edited by Teresa Elwes. London: Marshall Pickering, 1992.

One of the most important essays regarding the feminist critique of divine fatherhood and its use in theological language.

Wren, Brian. *What Language Shall I Borrow? God Talk in Worship and Male Response to Feminist Theology.* London: SCM, 1989.

A critical evaluation of the concept of divine power and kingship by a male feminist hymn writer. A valuable resource.

3. Challenging the Maleness of Christ: Feminist Approaches to Christology

Aldredge-Clanton, Jann. *In Search of the Christ-Sophia: An Inclusive Christology for Liberating Christians.* Mystic, Conn.: Twenty-Third Publications, 1995.

An introduction to inclusive and feminist Christology and alternative images of the Christ. Suitable for beginners. Aldredge-Clanton argues that using merely masculine language means reducing Christ to history without taking account of the resurrection and Christ's presence in the world today. She therefore suggests an inclusive Christology of the Christ-*Sophia* in order to recover the feminine in the second person of the Trinity. A Christology that is based on the risen Christ as well as the life of Jesus "lifts the incarnation out of the particularities of race, culture, and gender into a universal inclusiveness. The resurrected Christ-Sophia enables the transformation of human lives and of society. Those transformed through the image of the Christ-Sophia are empowered to a ministry of social justice through shared power. Such a ministry is based on the sacredness of all life and the hope for the resurrection of all creation. Aldredge-Clanton envisages a concept of Christology that integrates the masculine with the feminine through the life of Christ as a human male and the concept of divine wisdom as female. This is embodied in the church as a community in which male and female members can live in equal and inclusive relationships.

Brock, Rita Nakashima. *Journeys by Heart: A Christology of Erotic Power.* New York: Crossroad, 1988.

A feminist relational Christology taking into account experiences of sexual abuse and the abuse of power based on the exclusivity of the Christ symbol. One possible manifestation, but by far not the only one, of such erotic power is the life and ministry of Jesus. Brock also criticizes the significance given to the death of Christ. The image of the father who sacrifices his only son becomes the prototype of child abuse legitimized and condoned if done by human fathers. Brock criticizes patriarchal christologies for having been too focused on the male Christ and suggests a christological approach that is no longer centered on the person of Christ, but on the erotic power that comes into being within the Christa/community.

Brown, Joanne Carlson, and Carole E. Bohn, eds. *Christianity, Patriarchy and Abuse: A Feminist Critique.* New York: Pilgrim, 1990.

A collection of essays discussing the relationship between Christology and other aspects of the Christian tradition and sexual abuse and violence against women.

Fiorenza, Elisabeth Schüssler. *Jesus: Miriam's Child, Sophia's Prophet: Critical Issues in Feminist Christology.* London: SCM, 1995.

One of the most important discussions of feminist Christology, the person of Jesus, and his significance for women in the Christian tradition. Fiorenza explores the politics behind different forms of traditional Christology and proposes a rethinking of Jesus as divine wisdom in the context of the ekklesia of wo/men. Presumes some knowledge of feminist theological thinking and Fiorenza's terminology.

Grant, Jacqueline. *White Women's Christ and Black Women's Jesus: Feminist Christology and Womanist Response.* Atlanta: Scholars Press, 1989.

The author discusses sexism and the omission of black women's concerns and experiences from feminist discussions on Christology and introduces her own black feminist approach to the topic.

Heyward, Carter. *Speaking of Christ: A Lesbian Feminist Voice.* Cleveland: Pilgrim, 1989.

A lesbian feminist discussion of Christ, his maleness, and the use of the Christ-symbol in the Christian tradition and the contemporary church.

Hopkins, Julie. *Towards a Feminist Christology: Jesus of Nazareth, European Women and the Christological Crisis*. Kampen: Kok/Pharos, 1995.

An introduction to feminist theological critique of Christology written by a British Baptist minister. Easy to read and therefore suitable for beginners.

Johnson, Elizabeth A. *Consider Jesus: Waves of Renewal in Christology*. New York: Crossroad, 1990.

An in-depth evaluation of the life and work of Christ from a feminist perspective. Scholarly but readable.

Johnson, Elizabeth A. "Jesus, the Wisdom of God: A Biblical Basis for Non-Androcentric Christology," *Ephemerides Theologicae Lovaniensis* 61, no. 4 (1985): 261-94.

A vital study of the texts on which feminist theological reclaimings of wisdom Christology are based.

Ruether, Rosemary Radford. *To Change the World: Christology and Cultural Criticism*. London: SCM, 1981.

A good introduction into Ruether's critique of Christology and her reclaiming of the Jesus of the gospels. Ruether, the first feminist theologian to ask about the significance of Christ for doing theology from a feminist perspective, asks: Can a male savior save women? Her answer is that while Christology is the aspect of Christianity that has been used the most to exclude women from the power centers of Christianity, feminist theologians need to rediscover the humanity of Christ, his ministry, and message. Even though Christ was a male human being, he stood out against the culture and society of his time by speaking and ministering to women. Ruether criticizes high forms of Christology that concentrate on the divinity of Christ and suggests replacing them by a Christology from below that understands the earthly life and ministry of Christ as the precursor of a liberated cohumanity.

Schaberg, Jane. *The Illegitimacy of Jesus: A Feminist Theological Interpretation*. New York: Winston-Seabury, 1982.

A study of the incarnation narratives of the synoptic gospels, exploring the birth of Christ and the connected events using feminist biblical hermeneutics. A key text.

Snyder, Mary Hembrow. *The Christology of Rosemary Radford Ruether: A Critical Introduction.* Mystic, Conn.: Twenty-Third Publications, 1988.

Still the most comprehensive introduction and critical evaluation of Ruether's approach to feminist Christology.

Stevens, Maryanne, ed. *Reconstructing the Christ Symbol: Essays in Feminist Christology.* New York: Paulist, 1994.

A small collection of essays on feminist Christology by authors ranging from Eleanor McLaughlin to Jacqueline Grant. Useful as an introduction to different approaches.

Wilson-Kastner, Patricia. *Faith, Feminism and the Christ.* Philadelphia: Fortress, 1983.

One of the earlier texts of feminist Christology, but still a useful introduction to some of the key questions in the context of reclaiming the Christ-symbol. Wilson-Kastner understands Christ as "the agent of wholeness and reconciler of fragmentation in the world." Wilson-Kastner is among those feminist theologians who understand the Christian message of the cross as embodying those values that are also fundamental to feminism. Among these are love, wholeness, liberation, and reconciliation. They are realized through the life, death, and resurrection of Christ. Life in Christ means the completion of our being in the image of God as well as participation in God's being.

In Wilson-Kastner's view, the significance of Christ lies in his humanity, not in his maleness. Through the resurrection of Christ, the male-female dichotomy that runs through the church and through all of humanity has been overcome and healed. Christ therefore is the central symbol of inclusiveness, justice, and reconciliation.

4. Feminist Theological Anthropologies and Women's Bodies

Børrensen, Kari E. *Subordination and Equivalence: The Nature and Role of Women in Augustine and Aquinas.* Washington, D.C.: University Press of America, 1981.

A detailed study of the image of women in the works of Aquinas and Augustine, showing how their anthropologies have influenced and shaped theology and spirituality as well as women's experiences in the Western church.

Davaney, Sheila Greeve. "The Limits of the Appeal to Women's Experience," in *Shaping New Vision: Gender and Values in American Culture,* edited by Clarissa Atkinson, Constance Buchanan, and Margaret R. Miles. Ann Arbor: UMI Research Press, 1987.

A useful summary of the arguments in the debate about the significance and usefulness of the concept of "women's experience" among feminist theologians.

Graff, Ann O'Hara, ed. *In the Embrace of God: Feminist Approaches to Theological Anthropology.* Maryknoll, N.Y.: Orbis, 1995.

A wide-ranging collection of essays introducing different approaches to feminist theological anthropology.

Isherwood, Lisa, and Elizabeth Stuart. *Introducing Body Theology.* Sheffield: Sheffield Academic Press, 1998.

A well-written introduction to the topic of women's bodies in Christian theology and the importance of rethinking and re-writing traditional concepts. Written as part of an introductory series, but nevertheless challenging reading.

May, Melanie A. *A Body Knows: A Theopoetics of Death and Resurrection.* New York: Continuum, 1995.

One of the most challenging works of feminist theology, discussing body theology and the experience of suffering, illness, and death from a lesbian feminist perspective.

Moltmann-Wendel, Elisabeth. *I Am My Body: New Waves of Embodiment.* New York: Continuum, 1995.

An important contribution to the theological discussion of women's bodies and embodiment.

Saiving, Valerie. "The Human Situation: A Feminine View," in *Womanspirit Rising: A Feminist Reader in Religion,* edited by Carol P. Christ and Judith Plaskow. San Francisco: Harper & Row, 1979, pp. 25-42.

An important essay in the development of feminist theological anthropology and feminist theology in general.

5. Feminist Discourses of Sin and Salvation

Grey, Mary. *Redeeming the Dream: Feminism, Redemption and Christian Tradition.* London: SPCK, 1989.

This earlier discussion of concepts of redemption and salvation is still a useful introduction that is readable by both an academic and a non-academic audience.

Jantzen, Grace. "Feminism and Flourishing: Gender and Metaphor in Feminist Theology," *Feminist Theology* 10 (1995): 81-101.

Grace Jantzen suggests the metaphor "flourishing" as a means of describing a concept of salvation that can be viable for women. Traditional patriarchal concepts of salvation perceive the state of humanity to be corrupt and sinful and therefore in need of salvation through a male savior. The metaphor "flourishing," however, suggests that the original state of humanity is good and simply needs to be given the right conditions to grow, to develop and flourish in divine abundance. Such a theology of flourishing stands in contrast to an individualistic understanding of salvation and therefore lends itself to being at the heart of an ethics of social justice and commitment to those marginalized by society. Individualistic theologies of salvation are in danger of becoming depoliticized and introverted, and thereby supportive of the status quo of a patriarchal system of injustice, sexism, and racism.

Townes, E. M., ed. *A Troubling in My Soul: Womanist Perspectives on Evil and Suffering.* Maryknoll, N.Y.: Orbis, 1993.

A black feminist discussion of theological concepts of evil and suffering in Christian theology.

West, Angela. *Deadly Innocence: Feminism and the Mythology of Sin.* London: Cassell, 1995.

A critical discussion of structural concepts of sin used by feminist theologians arguing that feminist theologians often replace concepts and myths such as the fall of humanity with other equally destructive and dangerous myths that present an unrealistic concept of women's peacefulness and omit that women have also participated in evil and violence. *Deadly Innocence* is one of the most important critiques of a feminist concept of sin. West argues that it ultimately remains polarizing by viewing women as equal to men in every respect but sin. Women cannot merely be portrayed as innocent victims of sinful structures created by men; a feminist critique of history has to acknowledge the participation of women in events like the Holocaust. West proposes to treat ideological concepts such as the innocence of women with the same hermeneutical suspicion that is applied to the ideological distortions of patriarchy. She argues that white feminism "has given insufficient attention to the Fall as a symbol of the depth of human intolerance for difference" (p. 47). West points out a "secret symbiosis" between radical feminism and the patriarchal structures that are the targets of its critique.

A very angry but nevertheless important book. Good overviews of the arguments used by feminist theologians.

6. Rethinking Mary and the Saints

Bingemer, Maria Clara and Ivonne Gebara. *Mary, Mother of God, Mother of the Poor*. Maryknoll, N.Y.: Orbis, 1989.

A critical evaluation of the effect of some traditional Marian doctrines on the lives of Latin American women as well as a presentation of a constructive approach that shows the possibility of reclaiming Mary as a viable symbol for doing feminist theology in a Latin American context. The authors, two liberation theologians from Brazil, try to reclaim Mary as essentially a poor woman whose life becomes an important symbol of new humanity and liberation for poor women in Latin America and for the church as a whole.

Bingemer, Maria Clara, and Ivonne Gebara. "Mary," in *Mysterium Liberationis: Fundamental Concepts of Liberation Theology*, edited by Ignacio Ellacuría and Jon Sobrino, translated by Dinah Livingstone. London: Burns and Oates, 1989 and Maryknoll, N.Y.: Orbis, 1993, pp. 482-95.

A short summary of Bingemer and Gebara's approach to feminist reconstructions of Marian theology in a Latin American context.

Hamington, Maurice. *Hail Mary? The Struggle for Ultimate Womanhood in Catholicism*. London: Routledge, 1995.

A discussion of the role and significance of Mary in Roman Catholic theology and its impact on the lives of women and men in the Roman Catholic Church today.

Jegen, Carol Frances, ed. *Mary According to Women*. Kansas City, Mo.: Leaven, 1985.

A useful collection of essays representing different approaches to feminist Mariology.

Johnson, Elizabeth A. *Friends of God and Prophets: A Feminist Theological Reading of the Communion of Saints*. London: SCM, 1998.

An important evaluation of the concept of the church as the "communion of saints" from a feminist perspective. The most important feminist theological discussion of Mary and the saints.

Maeckelberghe, Els. *Desperately Seeking Mary: A Feminist Reappropriation of a Religious Symbol*. Kampen: Kok/Pharos, 1991.

A scholarly evaluation of different feminist theological approaches to the significance of Mary for doing feminist theology today and for the lives of women in the Christian churches. Maeckhelberghe's book provides the most comprehensive survey of feminist theological discussions of Marian theology, and argues for a reappropriation of Marian theology and symbolism in a way that allows for women to flourish within the church.

Ruether, Rosemary Radford. *Mary — The Feminine Face of the Church*. London: SCM, 1979.

One of the first feminist discussions of Marian doctrine and its impact on women's experiences. Ruether presents her own approach to reclaiming Mary for women in the church today. Aimed at both an academic and a non-academic audience.

Stuart, Elizabeth. *Spitting at Dragons: Towards a Feminist Theology of Sainthood*. London: Mowbray, 1996.

A highly readable attempt at reclaiming the idea of saints for doing feminist theology today; it tackles the issues from a slightly different angle than Johnson. An important book.

Warner, Marina. *Alone of All Her Sex: The Myth and the Cult of the Virgin Mary*. London: Quartet Books, 1978.

Not necessarily a feminist theological book itself, Warner's study has nevertheless influenced most feminist theologians' discussions of the impact of Marian doctrine, spirituality, and praxis on the lives and experiences of women throughout the Christian tradition and in the Roman Catholic Church today.

7. "Women Are Church":
Feminist Reconstructions of Ecclesiology

Behr-Sigel, Elisabeth. *The Ministry of Women in the Church*. Wheathampstead, U.K.: Oakwood, 1990.

The most important contribution to the debate about the ministry of women in the Orthodox churches.

Best, T. *Beyond Unity-in-Tension: Unity, Renewal and the Community of Women and Men*. Faith and Order Paper 138. Geneva: WCC, 1988.

A collection of different contributions to the debate about women's ministry among the different members of the World Council of Churches following the 1985 Sheffield Consultation.

Byrne, Lavinia. *Women at the Altar: The Ordination of Women in the Roman Catholic Church*. London: Mowbray, 1994.

A very accessible summary of the arguments presented by those in favor of the ordination of women to the priesthood in the Roman Catholic Church written from the perspective of a religious order member who has lived through the discussions on the topic since the Second Vatican Council.

Chittister, Joan D. *Women, Ministry and the Church*. New York: Paulist, 1983.

A very passionate discussion about the ordained and non-ordained ministry of women in the Roman Catholic Church.

Chittister, Joan D. *Winds of Change: Women Challenge the Church*. Kansas City, Mo.: Sheed & Ward, 1986.

An evaluation of the impact of Christian feminism and the debate about the ordination of women on the Roman Catholic Church.

Elizondo, Virgil, and Norbert Greinacher, eds. *Women in a Men's Church*. Concilium 134. Edinburgh: T. & T. CLark, 1980.

A *Concilium* volume containing a collection of essays regarding different aspects of the ministry and the experiences of women in the Roman Catholic Church and a variety of other denominations.

Fiorenza, Elisabeth Schüssler. *Discipleship of Equals: A Critical Feminist Ekklesia-logy of Liberation*. London: SCM, 1993.

A collection of Fiorenza's essays and papers presented at different stages throughout her career, showing the development of Fiorenza's theology of the "*ekklesia* of women" and women-church.

Fiorenza, Elisabeth Schüssler, and Mary Collins, eds. *Women Invisible in Church and Theology.* Concilium 182. Edinburgh: T. & T. Clark, 1985.

A *Concilium* volume containing a variety of short essays reflecting the development of feminist thinking on women's experiences regarding different aspects of theology and the church.

Fortune, Mary M. *Is Nothing Sacred? When Sex Invades the Pastoral Relationship.* San Francisco: Harper & Row, 1989.

An important discussion of sexuality and pastoral relationships, focusing on sexual abuse and harassment.

Furlong, Monica, ed. *Feminine in the Church.* London: SPCK, 1984.

A collection of essays on a variety of topics regarding women in the life of the church from a U.K. perspective.

Furlong, Monica, ed. *Mirror to the Church: Reflections on Sexism.* London: SPCK, 1988.

A collection of essays regarding the churches' refusal to ordain women and other aspects of women's experiences of sexist attitudes and policies in the church.

Furlong, Monica, ed. *A Dangerous Delight: Women and Power in the Church.* London: SPCK, 1991.

A collection of essays about a variety of topics regarding the themes of power and authority and their abuse in the church.

Graham, Elaine. *Transforming Practice: Pastoral Theology in an Age of Uncertainty.* London: Mowbray, 1996.

An evaluation of recent movements such as liberation theology, postmodernism, and feminism and their relevance for pastoral theology and the concept of pastoral agency. Not easy to read as it presumes knowledge of the movements discussed.

Gudorf, Christine. "The Power to Create: Sacraments and Men's Need to Birth," *Horizons* 14, no. 2 (1987): 296-309.

An interesting essay by a feminist theological ethicist showing the exclusion of women from the area of sacramental celebration and a possible way of reclaiming them for the life of the church.

Halsey, Margaret, and Elaine Graham, eds. *Life Cycles: Women and Pastoral Care.* London: SPCK, 1993.

A collection of essays about different aspects of pastoral care and women's experiences.

Hopkins, Julie, Angela Berlis, Hedwig Meyer-Wilmes, and Caroline Vander Stichele, eds. *Women Churches: Networking and Reflection in the European Context.* Yearbook of the European Society of Women in Theological Research. Kampen: Kok/Pharos, 1995.

A collection of essays on a variety of topics in the area of feminist reflections on the church from primarily European perspectives.

Martin, Fanny, Dorothea McEwan, and Lucy Tatman, eds. *Cymbals and Silences: Echoes from the First European Women's Synod.* London: Sophia Press, 1997.

This volume documents the keynote speeches as well as other events at the first European Women's Synod in Gmünden, Austria, in 1996.

Morley, Janet. *All Desires Known.* London: Women in Theology, 1988.

A collection of new prayers and liturgical resources introducing feminist Christian spirituality.

Northup, L., ed. *Women and Religious Ritual.* Washington, D.C.: Pastoral Press, 1993.

A collection of essays about different aspects of feminist transformations of worship in different churches and feminist liturgical communities.

Osiek, Carolyn, RSCJ. *Beyond Anger: On Being a Feminist in the Church.* New York: Paulist, 1986.

An account of Christian feminism from the perspective of a Roman Catholic religious sister. A good introduction.

Parvey, Constance, ed. *The Community of Men and Women in the Church: The Sheffield Report.* Geneva: WCC, 1983.

This collection of essays and papers documents the World Council of Churches' Sheffield Consultation on women and men in the church, an important milestone in the history of women in Protestant and Reformed churches.

Procter-Smith, Marjorie. *In Her Own Rite: Constructing Feminist Liturgical Tradition.* Nashville: Abingdon, 1990.

An introduction to feminist liturgical theology as a means of rethinking worship both in mainstream churches and feminist liturgical communities.

Procter-Smith, Marjorie, and J. Walton, eds. *Women in Worship: Interpretations of North American Diversity.* Louisville: Westminster/John Knox, 1993.

A collection of essays about different women's experiences of participating in worship in different churches and feminist liturgical communities.

Rhodes, Lynne Nell. *Co-Creation: A Feminist Vision of Ministry.* Philadelphia: Westminster, 1987.

An introduction to feminist approaches to ministry.

Ross, Susan A. *Extravagant Affections: Feminist Perspectives on Sacramental Theology.* New York: Continuum, 1998.

Probably the most comprehensive and scholarly study of the topic of sacramental theology from a feminist perspective, based on interviews with women in Roman Catholic parishes and on a study of traditional and contemporary sacramental theologies.

Ruether, Rosemary Radford. *Women-Church: Theology and Praxis of Feminist Liturgical Communities.* San Francisco: Harper & Row, 1988.

A key text introducing the theology and the lives of women-church communities as well as a number of feminist rituals celebrating different events in the lives of women commonly overlooked by the liturgical praxis of the churches.

Russell, Letty M. *Household of Freedom: Authority in Feminist Theology.* Philadelphia: Westminster, 1987.

A feminist discussion of the themes of power, authority, and their abuse in Christian churches, presenting an alternative feminist approach of shared power.

Russell, Letty M. *Church in the Round: Feminist Interpretation of the Church.* Louisville: Westminster/John Knox, 1993.

A key text presenting a feminist model of the church as a round-table community where everyone is welcome, from a feminist and Reformed perspective.

Smith, C. M. *Weaving the Sermon: Preaching in a Feminist Perspective.* Louisville: Westminster/John Knox, 1989.

An introduction to feminist approaches to preaching.

Stevenson, M. J., ed. *Through the Eyes of Women: Insights for Pastoral Care.* Minneapolis: Fortress, 1996.

A collection of essays introducing new feminist approaches to pastoral care and ministry and evaluating the impact of feminist theological thought on ministerial praxis in different churches.

Walton, Heather, and Susan Durber, eds. *Silence in Heaven: A Book of Women's Preaching.* London: SCM, 1994.

A collection of sermons preached by women, showing different approaches to preaching informed by feminist theology and praxis.

Watson, Natalie K. *Introducing Feminist Ecclesiologies.* Sheffield: Sheffield Academic Press, 2002.

A comprehensive introduction to the subject of feminist reflections on the church as a space that women need to claim and reclaim for their discourses of faith, worship, and justice.

8. Last Things or First? Feminists Questioning Eschatology

Adams, C., ed. *Ecofeminism and the Sacred.* New York: Continuum, 1993.

A collection of essays on ecofeminist theology.

Halkes, Catharina. *New Creation: Christian Feminism and the Renewal of the Earth.* London: SPCK, 1995.

An introduction to Christian ecofeminist theology and critique of eschatology.

Johnson, Elizabeth A. *Women, Earth and Creator Spirit.* New York: Paulist, 1993.

A scholarly discussion of pneumatology and eschatology from a feminist and ecological perspective.

Keller, Catherine. *Apocalypse Now and Then: A Feminist Approach to the End of the World.* Boston: Beacon, 1996.

A wide-ranging feminist discussion of "the last things," evaluating the Christian tradition and introducing new ways of thinking.

Primavesi, Anne. *From Apocalypse to Genesis: Ecology, Feminism and Christianity.* London: Burns & Oates, 1991.

A scholarly introduction to ecofeminist theology. Useful as an introduction to the topic.

Ruether, Rosemary Radford. *Gaia and God: An Ecofeminist Theology of Earth Healing.* London: SCM, 1992.

An introduction to Ruether's concept of ecofeminist theology.

Ruether, Rosemary Radford, ed. *Women Healing Earth: Third World Women on Ecology, Feminism, and Religion.* Maryknoll, N.Y.: Orbis, 1996.

A collection of essays by women from Asian, African, and Latin American contexts, discussing the importance of ecology and earth healing from their own feminist perspectives.

Towards a Feminist Theological Ethic

Andolsen, Barbara Hilkert, Christine E. Gudorf, and Mary D. Pellauer, eds. *Women's Consciousness, Women's Conscience: A Reader in Feminist Ethics.* Minneapolis: Winston, 1985.

A useful collection of essays introducing different approaches to feminist theological ethics. Useful as an introduction to the topic.

Borrowdale, Anne. *A Woman's Work: Changing Christian Attitudes.* London: SPCK, 1989.

A very readable discussion of the idea of service and self-denial and their impact on the lives of Christian women from a feminist perspective.

Cahill, Lisa Sowle. *Between the Sexes: Foundations for a Christian Ethics of Sexuality.* Philadelphia: Fortress, 1985.

An introduction to feminist Christian ethics.

Cahill, Lisa Sowle. *Sex, Gender and Christian Ethics.* Cambridge: Cambridge University Press, 1996.

An introduction to questions and issues of sexuality and gender and their relevance for Christian ethics. An important contribution to the debate.

Cannon, K. *Black Womanist Ethics.* Atlanta: Scholars Press, 1988.

An introduction to theological ethics from a black feminist perspective.

Daly, L. K., ed. *Feminist Theological Ethics: A Reader.* Louisville: Westminster/John Knox, 1994.

A collection of essays introducing different approaches to feminist theological ethics.

Fortune, Mary M. *Sexual Violence: The Unmentionable Sin.* New York: Pilgrim, 1983.

A feminist discussion of issues of sexual abuse and violence against women aimed at both theologians and those engaged in pastoral ministry.

Fortune, Mary M. *Keeping the Faith: Questions and Answers for the Abused Woman.* San Francisco: Harper & Row, 1987.

An introduction to the feminist ethical discussion of sexual abuse of women in family and pastoral situations.

Gudorf, Christine E. *Body, Sex and Pleasure: Reconstructing Christian Sexual Ethics.* Cleveland: Pilgrim, 1994.

An introduction to feminist theological ethics of sexuality.

Harrison, Beverly Wildung. *Making the Connections: Essays in Feminist Social Ethics,* edited by Carol S. Robb. Boston: Beacon, 1985.

A collection of essays by one of the pioneers and key thinkers of feminist theological ethics in the liberal tradition.

Legge, Marilyn J. *The Grace of Difference: A Canadian Feminist Theological Ethic.* Atlanta: Scholars Press, 1992.

An introduction to feminist theological ethics from a Canadian perspective.

Miller-McLemore, Bonnie J. *Also a Mother: Work and Family as Theological Dilemma.* Nashville: Abingdon, 1994.

A discussion of issues of motherhood, reproduction, and women's work as issues of feminist theological ethics.

Parsons, Susan F. *Feminism and Christian Ethics.* Cambridge: Cambridge University Press, 1996.

A scholarly introduction to different approaches to feminist ethical thinking that provides a number of useful summaries.

Patrick, Anne E. *Liberating Conscience: Feminist Explorations in Catholic Moral Theology.* London: SCM, 1996.

A feminist discussion of Roman Catholic moral theology, contrasting patriarchal and feminist paradigms and emphasizing the importance of conscience and social justice.

Welch, Sharon D. *A Feminist Ethic of Risk.* Minneapolis: Fortress, 1990.

An introduction to feminist ethics from a Christian perspective.

Feminist Theologies from Different Contexts

Aquino, Maria Pilar, ed. *Our Cry for Life: Feminist Theology from Latin America.* Maryknoll, N.Y.: Orbis, 1995.

A collection of essays introducing feminist theology in a Latin American context.

Dietrich, Gabriele. *Women's Movement in India: Conceptual and Religious Reflections.* Bangalore: Breakthrough Publications, 1988.

An introduction of feminist theology in the context of the Indian subcontinent.

Esser, Annette, and Luise Schottroff, eds. *Feminist Theology in a European Context.* Kampen: Kok/Pharos, 1993.

This *Yearbook of the European Society of Women in Theological Research* introduces different approaches and topics relevant to doing theology in the context of different European countries.

Fabella, Virginia, and Sun Ai Lee Park, eds. *We Dare to Dream: Doing Theology as Asian Women*. Maryknoll, N.Y.: Orbis, 1990.

A collection of essays introducing the work of feminist theologians from a variety of Asian countries.

Fabella, Virginia, and S. Torres, eds. *Irruption of the Third World: Challenge to Theology*. Maryknoll, N.Y.: Orbis, 1983.

A collection of essays by feminist theologians from a number of different Third World countries.

Hyun-Kyung, Chung. *Struggle to Be the Sun Again: Introducing Asian Women's Theology*. London: SCM, 1991.

A Korean feminist theology, using elements of traditional Korean religion in order to create a theology relevant to the experiences of Korean women. The author draws on elements of traditional Korean religion and culture in order to re-write Christian theology in a way that helps Asian women make sense of their own experiences of suffering, for example, as "comfort women" forced to provide sex for American soldiers during the Second World War, or the experience of the atrocities committed during the Japanese occupation of Korea. Chung Hyun-Kyung uses the concept of *han,* meaning resentment or anger, an important element of traditional Korean religion, in order to make theological sense of the situation of women in Korea. Hyun-Kyung attracted public attention through her contribution to the discussions at the Assembly of the World Council of Churches in Canberra in 1993 when she approached the topic "Come, Holy Spirit, renew the face of the earth . . ." through using elements of traditional shamanistic spirituality.

Isasi-Díaz, Ada María. *En la Lucha: A Hispanic Women's Liberation Theology*. Minneapolis: Fortress, 1993.

An introduction to theology from the perspective of Latina women. Isasi-Díaz argues that Latinas have become dissatisfied with their attempts to participate in North American feminist theology because of its inability to deal with differences and its failure to find ways of enabling Latinas to contribute to the reconsideration of the core concepts of theology. Hispanic women come to understand themselves as living within sinful and destructive structures. To change these structures is the aim of the struggle that *mujerista* theology advocates. The reason for choosing the daily lives of Hispanic women as the hermeneutical and epistemological framework of *mujerista* theology is to rescue them from being rendered unimportant or insignificant.

Isasi-Díaz, Ada María. *Mujerista Theology: A Theology for the Twenty-First Century.* Maryknoll, N.Y.: Orbis, 1996.

An introduction to theological reflection on the lives of Hispanic women.

Isasi-Díaz, Ada María, and Y. Tanango. *Hispanic Women, Prophetic Voice in the Church: Toward a Hispanic Women's Liberation Theology.* Minneapolis: Fortress, 1993.

An introduction to theology done by Hispanic women in both English and Spanish.

Katoppo, Marianne. *Compassionate and Free: An Asian Women's Theology.* Maryknoll, N.Y.: Orbis, 1980.

An introduction to theology in the context of Asian women's lives and experiences.

King, Ursula, ed. *Feminist Theology from a Third World Perspective: A Reader.* London: SPCK, 1994.

A collection of essays introducing feminist theologies from different Third World countries.

Oduyoye, Mercy Amba. *Hearing and Knowing: Theological Reflections on Christianity in Africa.* Maryknoll, N.Y.: Orbis, 1986.

An introduction to feminist theology from the perspectives of African women.

Oduyoye, Mercy Amba. *Who Will Roll the Stone Away?* Geneva: WCC, 1990.

Theology from the perspectives of African women.

Oduyoye, Mercy Amba, and Virginia Fabella, eds. *With Passion and Compassion: Third World Women Doing Theology.* Maryknoll, N.Y.: Orbis, 1988.

A collection of essays introducing different types of feminist theology from the perspectives of women in Third World countries.

Ortega, Ofelia, ed. *Women's Visions: Theological Reflection, Celebration, Action.* Geneva: WCC, 1995.

A collection of essays introducing women's theological reflections from different countries throughout the world.

Russell, Letty M., ed. *Inheriting Our Mothers' Gardens: Feminist Theology in Third World Perspective*. Philadelphia: Westminster, 1988.

A collection of essays introducing feminist theology and women's spiritualities from different Third World countries.

Tamez, Elsa, ed. *Through Her Eyes: Women's Theology in Latin America*. Maryknoll, N.Y.: Orbis, 1989.

An introduction to feminist theology from a Latin American context.

Thistlethwaite, Susan Brooks, and M. P. Engel, eds. *Lift Every Voice: Constructing Christian Theologies from the Underside*. San Francisco: Harper & Row, 1990.

A collection of essays introducing feminist theologies on the margins.

von Wartenberg-Potter, B. *We Will Not Hang Our Harps on the Willows*. Geneva: WCC, 1987.

An collection of essays introducing women's spiritualities and theologies from different churches in the World Council of Churches.

Williams, Delores. *Sisters in the Wilderness*. Maryknoll, N.Y.: Orbis, 1993.

An introduction to black feminist theology. Williams is one of the younger representatives of womanist theology. She defines womanist theology as rooted in the history of the survival and resistance of black women and the context of the black family and community. Racism, sexism, and classism are expressions of the same system of multiple oppression from which black women have suffered and still suffer. The perpetrators of this multiple oppression are equally diverse; they include white women as well as black and white men. Williams defines the multilayered oppression of black women as the hermeneutical norm by which the appropriateness of theological concepts and readings of scriptural texts are to be judged. Williams understands the story of Hagar and Sarah as the biblical paradigm for the experiences of black women. Hagar is exposed to racism and domestic violence at the hands of her mistress Sarah, who eventually casts her and her son out into the wilderness. There she encounters God, who sends her back to her mistress only to suffer further violence and eventual expulsion. God, as described in this story, remains an ambivalent figure who cannot be seen as being entirely on the side of Hagar, who represents black women. This ambivalent experience calls for black women to draw on their own history and experiences as well as African traditions in order to develop their own salvific and liberating theology. Williams understands the cross as a symbol of evil and the rejection of

Jesus and his ministry of love and life. It symbolizes the risk of suffering and death as a potential danger for anyone involved in the struggle for freedom and justice. Williams rejects traditional interpretations of the atonement and the redemptive value of the death of Jesus, but argues that it is the life of Jesus and his commitment to a ministry of justice and communities of right relation that is ultimately life-giving for black women.

Lesbian Feminist Theologies

Heyward, Carter. *Our Passion for Justice: Images of Power, Sexuality, and Liberation.* Cleveland: Pilgrim, 1984.

A collection of essays giving an overview of Heyward's work as a theologian, writer, and priest.

Heyward, Carter. *Touching Our Strength: The Erotic as Power and the Love of God.* San Francisco: Harper & Row, 1989.

An introduction to lesbian feminist theology. The author describes the process of "coming out of the closet" as an empowering to right and good relationships not only among people, but also with God. Heyward envisages God as a relational matrix who embodies justice and relational power in mutual relation: "God is our relational power. God is born in this relational power. God is becoming our power insofar as we are giving birth to this sacred Spirit in the quality of our lives in relation, the authenticity of our mutuality and equality, the strength of our relational matrix" (p. 24). God is embodied in relationships and the relational selves involved in them. The erotic is the sacred power in which God is experienced in human relationships of justice and mutuality and through making connections. This also involves affirming sexuality and sexual pleasure as powerful and intrinsically good.

Heyward, Carter. *Staying Power: Reflections on Gender, Justice, and Compassion.* Cleveland: Pilgrim, 1995.

A discussion of gender and justice from a lesbian feminist perspective.

Hunt, Mary E. *Fierce Tenderness: A Feminist Theology of Friendship.* New York: Crossroad, 1991.

A theological discussion of friendship and lesbian relationships that introduces friendship as a new paradigm of human relationships.

Jantzen, Grace M. "Off the Straight and Narrow: Toward a Lesbian Theology," *Theology and Sexuality* 3 (1995): 58-76.

A short introduction to lesbian feminist theology by a British feminist theologian and philosopher. Jantzen suggests a "transgressive theology." Lesbian feminists perceive themselves as a disruptive community within the shared praxis of the church. Lesbian feminist theology has to be embodied thinking of sexual subjects. Only then will the dominating discourse of heterosexual theology be disrupted. Embodied thinking is authentic to one of the most central truths of the Christian faith: the incarnation. The presence of lesbian feminists in theology challenges theologians to reconsider Christian theologies of creation from the perspective of multiplicity and diversity within the community. It ultimately leads to a reconceptualization of God in order to free God from the limitations of heterosexual theological thinking. A straight God, according to Jantzen, has been the creation of a straight and narrow mind.

Stuart, Elizabeth. *Just Good Friends: Towards a Lesbian and Gay Theology of Relationships.* London: Mowbray, 1995

A feminist theological discussion of friendship and sexual relationships.

Post-Christian Feminisms

Caron, C. *To Make and Make Again: Feminist Ritual Thealogy.* New York: Crossroad, 1993.

An introduction to feminist goddess spirituality.

Christ, Carol P. *Laughter of Aphrodite: Reflections on a Journey to the Goddess.* San Francisco: Harper & Row, 1987.

A collection of essays on post-Christian spirituality and the reinvention of the Goddess. Carol Christ understands feminist goddess spirituality as a combination of the elements of pre-Christian female-centered religion with contemporary ideas and experiences. Discourses of the Goddess are about the affirmation of female power in nature that has been subdued and perceived as threatening in patriarchal religions such as Judaism or Christianity.

Daly, Mary. *Beyond God the Father: Toward a Philosophy of Women's Liberation.* London: Women's Press, 1973.

Daly's first post-Christian book, in which she discusses why she left Christianity behind in order to work towards the liberation of women. Using Tillich's concept of "correlation," she urges women to leave behind Christolatry and the idolatry of God the Father. Religion for Daly is patriarchy's most powerful means of self-legitimization. Through religion men have silenced women into non-being. Leaving religion and its institutions behind is therefore an essential step of liberation into the New Being, another Tillichian term applied to women. Instead, women are to enter "sisterhood," which is both anti-church and the cosmic covenant.

Daly, Mary. *Gyn/Ecology: The Metaethics of Radical Feminism.* London: Women's Press, 1978.

A series of case studies show how religion and Christianity in particular have been the means of oppressing women throughout history and therefore need to be left behind by women in order to work for their own liberation from male power. Women's liberation, for Daly, begins with the exorcism of patriarchy. In order to exorcise patriarchy, Daly shows the omnipresence of the destructive forces of patriarchy that destroy women's lives through, for example, African genital mutilation and the European witch-hunt, but also through Nazi medicine and American gynecology. This exorcism is not only to affect religion, though religion for Daly is the most powerful expression of the patriarchal abuse of power, but it is also to affect language: Daly proposes the invention of a new feminist language that she has outlined in her new *Intergalactic Wickedary of the English Language.* One of the most compelling aspects of Daly's post-Christian radical feminism is its similarity to the Christianity Daly claims to have left behind. This is combined with an explicit lack of historical awareness. History for Daly is the history of patriarchy and its oppression of women. Daly denies that women throughout this history have been able to make their own spaces for their own forms of spirituality. That essentially denies centuries of women's history within the church and attempts to replace women's existing traditions within the church with an ideal of women's sisterhood that bears the same potential to be transformed into either destructive anarchy or a restrictive institution like the patriarchal church. Daly's concept of "sisterhood" remains essentially disembodied and obsessed with the destructive forces of patriarchy that attack women's bodies, overlooking the transformative presence of women's bodies that embody the body of Christ. Therefore her project of sisterhood as the post-patriarchal anti-church cannot be of use to the feminist transformation of theology, as it essentially remains at the stage of deconstruction without taking account of the constructive power already present in women's being church.

Daly, Mary. *Pure Lust: Elemental Feminist Philosophy.* London: Women's Press, 1984.

Daly's third post-Christian book introduces her new women-centered philosophy.

Daly, Mary. *Quintessence: Realizing the Archaic Future. A Radical Elemental Manifesto.* Boston: Beacon, 1998.

Daly's most recent book envisages a feminist, post-patriarchal society in which women have moved to a newly found continent where life is shaped and defined by women, and where men have essentially disappeared.

Goldenberg, Naomi. *Changing of the Gods: Feminism and the End of Traditional Religions.* Boston: Beacon, 1979.

A post-Jewish discussion of goddess spirituality and new images of the divine.

Hampson, Daphne. *Theology and Feminism.* Oxford: Blackwell, 1990.

A discussion of Hampson's reason to leave Christianity behind on the grounds that it is unethical. Hampson outlines the new gender-free religion that she envisages as replacing the kind of liberal Christianity she has left behind. Hampson, originally a historian, had for many years been a campaigner for the ordination women in the Church of England. She later decided to leave Christianity on the grounds of its being irredeemably patriarchal. She proposes instead a spirituality that is free of gendered structures and has at its heart the fundamental equality of women and men. Christianity, in her view, must be understood and rejected as a myth that is not only untrue, but essentially immoral and superstitious. The focal point of this rejection of Christianity is the prominence given to the person of Christ and the transcendent monotheism that is used as a means of a culturally conditioned patriarchal religion in order to subdue and exclude women. Hampson describes the damaging effect of transcendent monotheism as creating structures of "insiders" and "outsiders," those who are like and those who are seen as "other." A religion that ascribes supreme importance to one male human being cannot contain any salvific value for women. Hampson argues that Christianity is a historical religion that makes it essentially sexist and therefore no longer viable for feminists. What Hampson proposes instead is not atheism or agnosticism, but a "new realist theism" based on observations of the presence of power and love in the world. The theism that Hampson proposes is "gender-free." According to Hampson, feminist theory provides Western religion with paradigms that will enable a reconceptualization of the divine, away from the masculinist conception of a gendered dichotomous worldview to a concept of interconnected centered selves in relation. The truth of Christianity for Hampson is related to its ethical viability. Christianity as Hampson perceives it is essentially heteronomous, while the values of feminism are based on human independence and autonomy. While Hampson argues that Christianity has become untenable, this does not lead into the void, but to the development of a new feminist spirituality and ethics. Such a new feminist spirituality and ethics have to take account of and proclaim the subjectivity of women. Any expression of a religion that fails to reflect this sense of women's subjectivity is inevitably irrelevant, as it is irredeemably patriarchal.

Hampson, Daphne. *After Christianity*. London: SCM, 1996.

A further development of Hampson's post-Christian philosophy, ethics, and spirituality.

Long, Ashphodel. *In a Chariot Drawn by Lion: The Search for the Female Deity*. London: Women's Press, 1992.

An introduction to feminist goddess spirituality by a British Jewish feminist.

Morton, Nelle. *The Journey Is Home*. Boston: Beacon, 1985.

One of the classic key texts of post-Christian feminist goddess spirituality.

Raphael, Melissa. *Thealogy and Embodiment: The Post-Patriarchal Reconstruction of Female Sacrality*. Sheffield: Sheffield Academic Press, 1996.

A discussion of different types of post-Christian and goddess spiritualities and their usability for the development of a spiritual feminism that takes the sacrality of women's bodies seriously.

Starhawk. *The Spiral Dance: A Rebirth of the Ancient Religion of the Great Goddess*. San Francisco: Harper & Row, 1979.

An introduction to goddess feminism and Wicca. Starhawk, a self-declared witch, describes the goddess religion that she practices as bringing together the spiritual and the political. She distinguishes it from traditional religions by saying that Wicca is not a religion based on dogma or a holy book, but rather on ritual, on experience, and on practices that change consciousness and waken power from within. The concept of the Goddess prevalent in goddess feminism must not be seen as a reverse form of traditional male theistic religion, but rather as a symbol of immanence: "She represents the divine embodied in nature, in human beings, in the flesh. The Goddess is not one image but many — a constellation of forms and associations — earth, air, fire, water, moon and star, sun, flower and seed, willow and apple, black, red, white, Maiden, Mother, and Crone. . . . Yet the femaleness of the Goddess is primary not to denigrate the male, but because it represents bringing life into the world, valuing the world" (p. 9).

Stone, Merlin. *When God Was a Woman.* New York: Dial, 1976.

An introduction to the reinvention of goddess spirituality as a resource for women's spiritual journeys.

Critical Discussions of Feminist Theologies and Their Methodologies

Chopp, Rebecca. *The Power to Speak: Feminism, Language, God.* New York: Crossroad, 1992.

An introduction to post-structuralist feminist theology. Important, but not for beginners. Chopp presumes knowledge of feminist and liberation theology as well as of post-structuralist thought.

Chopp, Rebecca S., and Sheila G. Davaney. *Horizons in Feminist Theology: Identity, Tradition, and Norms.* Minneapolis: Fortress, 1997

A collection of essays that discuss the methodologies used by feminist theologians in the light of recent developments in feminist theory and theological methodology. Most of the essays are not suitable for beginners as they presume a significant amount of knowledge in feminist theory and different approaches to feminist theology.

Fulkerson, Mary McClintock. *Changing the Subject: Women's Discourses and Feminist Theology.* Minneapolis: Fortress, 1994.

A post-structuralist analysis of feminist theology, its methodologies, and sources. Not easy to read, but a vital contribution to the debate. Fulkerson proposes a critique of the methodologies used by feminist theologies that suggests that feminist theology has only taken into account *some* women's discourses of faith, but left out those that are meaningful to women outside the academic white middle-class context in which much feminist theology still takes place.

Hampson, Daphne, ed. *Swallowing a Fishbone: Feminist Theologians Debate Christianity.* London: SPCK, 1996.

This book is the result of a discussion of a group of feminist theologians about the relevance of Christianity for women. Some of the articles are not easy to read, but it is nevertheless an interesting and challenging contribution to the debate about whether or not Christianity and feminist thinking can be reconciled with each other.

Heine, Susanne. *Women and Early Christianity: Are the Feminist Scholars Right?* London: SCM, 1986.

A critical assessment of feminist discussions of early Christianity, focusing on a "lack of method" by feminist theologians.

Heine, Susanne. *Matriarchs, Goddesses, and Images of God.* Philadelphia: Fortress, 1989.

An evaluation of feminist theology from the point of view of a systematic theologian.

Hogan, Linda. *From Women's Experience to Feminist Theology.* Sheffield: Sheffield Academic Press, 1995.

A discussion of the use of liberation theology, the concept of "women's experience," and the notion of praxis — an interesting and readable introduction to feminist theological methodology and a critical appraisal of the developments of liberal feminist theology.

Holloway, Richard, ed. *Who Needs Feminism?: Men Respond to Sexism in the Church.* London: SPCK, 1991.

A collection of essays by male scholars assessing the impact of feminist theology on theological discourses in Britain and worldwide.

Hunt, Mary E. "Feminist Liberation Theology: The Development of Method in Construction." Doctoral dissertation. Ann Arbor: UMI, 1980.

Unpublished Ph.D. thesis, but still very useful in terms of the relationship between feminist theology and liberation theology. Hunt was the first author to make the connection between liberation theology and feminist theology and praxis.

Martin, Francis. *The Feminist Question: Feminist Theology in the Light of the Christian Tradition.* Grand Rapids: Eerdmans and Edinburgh: T. & T. Clark, 1994.

An evaluation of liberal feminist theology from the perspective of Roman Catholic moral theology and Christian orthodoxy. Not easy to read and very limited in its account of what feminist theology is and aims to achieve.

Vuola, Elina. *Limits of Liberation: Praxis as Method in Latin American Liberation Theology and Feminist Theology.* Helsinki: The Finnish Academy of Science and Letters, 1997.

This book proposes a critical dialogue between feminist and liberation theologies that intends a thorough critique of liberation theology as omitting the experiences of Latin American women from its concept of praxis. The book is not intended for beginners but presumes a certain amount of knowledge of both feminist and liberation theology and their respective methodologies.

Welch, Sharon D. *Communities of Resistance and Solidarity: A Feminist Theology of Liberation.* Maryknoll, N.Y.: Orbis, 1985.

This book, which is not easy to read for beginners, seeks to apply Foucault's ideas on the ubiquity of power to feminist approaches to Christian praxis.

Woodhead, Linda. "Spiritualising the Sacred: A Critique of Feminist Theology," *Modern Theology* 13, no. 2 (1997): 191-212.

A critical discussion of feminist theology, its methods, and achievements by a religious studies scholar and ethicist.